COOL TO BE KIND

Published by ECW Press
2120 Queen Street East, Suite 200, Toronto, Ontario, Canada M4E 1E2

NATIONAL LIBRARY OF CANADA CATALOGUING IN PUBLICATION

Cool to be kind: random acts of kindness and how to commit them /
Val Litwin . . . [et al.].

ISBN 1-55022-652-5

1. Kindness. I. Litwin, Val

BJ1533.K5C66 2004   177'.7   C2004-900107-8

SOME NAMES HAVE BEEN CHANGED TO RESPECT PRIVACY

Editing: Joy Gugeler
Cover and Text Design: Tania Craan
Production and Typesetting: Mary Bowness
Printing: St. Joseph Print Group

This book is set in Minion.

The publication of *Cool to Be Kind* has been generously supported
by the Canada Council, the Ontario Arts Council, the Government
of Canada through the Book Publishing Industry
Development Program. **Canada**

DISTRIBUTION
CANADA: Jaguar Book Group, 100 Armstrong Avenue, Georgetown, ON, L7G 5S4
UNITED STATES: Independent Publishers Group, 814 North Franklin Street,
Chicago, Illinois 60610

PRINTED AND BOUND IN CANADA

ECW PRESS
ecwpress.com

COOL TO BE KIND

RANDOM ACTS AND
HOW TO COMMIT THEM

VAL LITWIN, BRAD STOKES,
ERIK HANSON, AND CHRIS BRATSETH

ECW PRESS

We would like to dedicate this book to friends and family whose infinite kindness, love, and compassion allowed us to realize a grand dream; we took over your homes, borrowed your cars, ate your food, and still you supported us: Judy and Devon Stokes-Bennett, Colleen and Dave Bratseth, Michael and Grania Litwin, Wayne and Maggie Hanson, Jamie Beuthin and, of course, Lorraine Wilson. Special love and thanks to our superhuman support crew of Jonathon Bratseth, David Crow, Kelly Seaman, and Dan Cox.

FOREWORD
CATHERINE RYAN HYDE

The day I first got wind of the Kindness Crew, I was in a nondescript hotel room listening to CNN. I was travelling extensively, and continuously, to promote *Pay It Forward* — both my book and the subsequent film. I was likely getting ready to attend a city-wide read of the book, or was on my way to address a school on behalf of the Pay It Forward Foundation. Cities were declaring themselves "The Pay It Forward City" of their state, mayors were proclaiming "Pay It Forward Day" in their towns. The events and ideas were staggering; I had never seen a groundswell quite like this.

CNN Headline News droned in the background as I ironed an outfit for the event. I snapped to attention when I heard someone say "Pay It Forward." I sat and waited until it cycled around again. There they were: Chris, Val, Erik, and Brad. They introduced themselves as ExtremeKindness.com. Erik played little riffs on his trombone as they stopped total strangers on the street to serve them food at outdoor tables. They were out there paying it forward, and planning a coast-to-coast tour. I would have to drop them a line.

A few months later they were hugging me, one by one

(and all on videotape) at the airport in Halifax, Nova Scotia. I was at the tail end of a long Pay It Forward run myself. I'd come from a city-wide read of the book in New Jersey, several days in New York, and a trip by train upstate to keynote a Pay It Forward conference at a state university. After briefly joining the Crew in Nova Scotia, I would be on to Toronto to speak to the Ontario Hospital Association on behalf of Pay It Forward Canada. My life was full of these tributes to real-life Pay It Forward heroes, but these heroes were different somehow; they would be the ones who really stood out.

After a few years of The Pay It Forward Movement, I find I have tons of friends I've never actually met in places I've never actually been. People find my email address on the web and share ideas. I have pen pals all over the world. When I toured Australia and New Zealand on behalf of Pay It Forward, I was able to hook up with two friends I'd never met. It was the same in Beaverton, Oregon and in Halifax, Nova Scotia.

The Crew and I were joined at the kick-off press conference by my Internet friend and pen pal, Barry. Quiet and reserved as he seemed, I'll be darned if he didn't don a paper chef's hat, load up on fresh-baked cookies provided by the Citadel Hotel, and hit the cold streets with us. We gave cookies to strangers walking by on the street, walked up to people in cars. We had scarves from the hotel with Pay It Forward logos on them, which we gave to homeless people. (Why are they always so easy to find? In just about any city, when I've been part of any street-based Pay It Forward plan to aid the homeless with food or warm clothes, we never have trouble finding them. I long for the day when we go out to provide for the homeless and just can't seem to locate any.) They had cookies that day, and scarves for a long time to come. Later I would receive a letter from Barry, telling me what a wonderful and memorable day that had been for him. Funny how you set out to save those less fortunate than yourself and by the time it's all over, you wonder who saved whom.

There were more adventures, of course. I'd love to tell you about Spa Day, how it felt to walk down a busy street in Nova Scotia, at temperatures well below zero, in an icy wind, accompanied by a group of young men wearing white terry bathrobes and flip-flops. Oh, yes, and did I mention they were carrying a sofa? But they'll tell you about all of those adventures themselves, quite capably, before this book is over. In their own words, as it should be.

After three days of changing the world (albeit in small ways) as a newly formed team, we all sat in the hotel restaurant having breakfast. Through the window we could see the hotel sign that advertised the temperature. It was hovering around zero and it was snowing, hard, blanketing the Citadel high on the neighbouring hill. There were predictions that the snow might turn to rain before I had to fly out. A person could get snowed in and I didn't want that, did I? I wanted to go home. Didn't I?

Erik had just gotten back from giving a free surfing lesson. The guys were explaining how cranberry juice had been a big part of staying healthy after so much hard time on the road. We talked about this book, just a good idea at the time, and about the upcoming U.S. tour. Kelly had an idea for a Pay It Forward documentary. Their tour was almost done; tentative energy hung in the air. You know the stuff I mean: "It was great, but it's almost over. It's almost time to return to our lives the way they were before this happened. What was that like again?"

I had to go back to my room and work on my speech for Toronto. Throughout the morning, one by one, the guys came to my room to exchange a few last thoughts and say goodbye.

I realized that I envied them for what they'd experienced; this tour had been a complete life-changer for them and I'd missed the vast majority of it. They'd go on to Newfoundland, and I was on my way home.

My association with the Crew didn't stop there, though. It was shortly after the end of the tour that I got a follow-up letter from Chris. "On a tragic note, someone has pirated our Web site and put it up for auction on eBay." I looked on eBay, and sure enough, there it was: Extemekindness.com. I remembered my first glimpse of them on CNN saying in unison, "and we are . . . ExtremeKindness.com!" That's *who they were*. Nobody should be able to take that away.

I bid on it, hoping to win it and give it back, but the pirate threw us a curve. He ended the auction early and cancelled all the bids. In a panic, I contacted him. It turned out he was getting better offers directly, off eBay, so I tried to be one of those better offers. It didn't seem to be working, though. The price was getting dangerously close to the "more than I can manage" level.

I called Erik and said, "I don't know if it'll work or

not, but I tried. I've done everything I can do." We would just have to wait.

But, while I was waiting, it hit me. Maybe I hadn't done everything it was in my power to do; I hadn't told the pirate why it was so important, why I wanted the site so badly. He didn't even know who Val, Chris, Brad, and Erik were. He knew nothing about the Crew. Would he even care? I had no idea. But I also had nothing to lose, so I sent him the following message by email. I saved it, so this is verbatim:

> *Let me just tell you why it is I want the site so badly. Maybe it won't make any difference, but I have to at least try. The guys that owned this site are the Kindness Crew. They quit their jobs, ran themselves ragged to get funding, gave up their rented homes, and travelled all across Canada doing acts of kindness. They were inspired by my book,* Pay It Forward. *The reason the site is so hot is because of their good work, because of the really positive content they created. It made people feel good. Of course, the site will cool down when people realize it doesn't belong to them. Maybe your other buyers are smart enough to figure it out, maybe not. But, just so you know . . . You say you are an ethical man. As far as I know, I am the only one trying to buy the site to give it back to the Kindness Crew. You would make a good profit, and there is a lot of good karma involved. If you care about stuff like that. Maybe you don't. Maybe an extra hundred means more to you. If so, maybe I could even cough up an extra hundred. I*

just wanted to take one last chance, to see what kind of guy you are. This Web site means everything to the Kindness Crew. And I really love those guys. I spent three days with them on their tour in Nova Scotia. They are the best. I am trying to buy this as a present for them. If that makes any difference. I just thought I'd take one last shot, and say my piece. Thanks.

He responded with a private auction, selling me the site. I guess even Internet pirates are moved by this stuff.

There's really only one exaggeration in that letter — when I said they were inspired by my book. These guys don't need inspiration; they are inspiration. I think the book and movie may have played some small role and it's great they used the phrase to deputize others to increase acts of kindness in the world, but any attempt to take credit for their actions would misrepresent us both. I didn't teach these guys to be kind, nor did I need to. The rest of what I said is true: they are the best and it's easy to love people who put so much love into the world.

The point of the story is that what started out as the least kind, least altruistic note of the entire Kindness Crew project became another of its real triumphs. What could have been a terrible lesson in human nature had a happy ending. Kindness won out again.

I have a couple of souvenirs from the tour: a warm knit hat, and a scarf with a Pay It Forward logo, a photo of me doing a live national CBC television interview on a freezing Halifax street corner while Val, dressed in just a bathrobe and toque, gave me a shoulder massage, and the sense that I was brought in to be a tiny part of it all.

The Crew and I still keep in touch and though I missed most of this life-changing tour, now I don't mind. I feel better after reading their first-person accounts in this book. It's a great feeling, as if someone opened a door and let me in, let me experience it for myself, helped me see "what it was really like." This book magically allows me to feel I was there for all of it. It will work for you, too. In fact, after you read this book, you might find that you *are* there, experiencing it for yourself. Maybe your own kindness project will be smaller than what you'll read in this book, but it doesn't matter. There's no wrong way to commit acts of kindness; a little bit from all of us would change the world. Let yourself be inspired, you might be surprised.

PREFACE — CHRIS

At noon the nurses called us to her room. Devon, Brad's sister, was already inside stroking her mother's forehead. Brad moved to the other side of the bed and held Judy's weak hand. Her breathing was shallow, a rattling in the back of her throat. Her skin was pale and her body emaciated. Death was moments away. Her breath slowed, then stopped. Silence inhabited the sterile room.

We looked at each other uncertainly — we'd never done this before. Brad groaned in pain and collapsed by Judy's side. We faced the reality of the situation: how were her children going to cope? Brad and Devon had no family — no father, no grandparents — we *were* their family.

Silently, I promised Judy that her life would move me to make a difference. Throughout our years in university together, Judy was a mother figure to all of us, her affection and advice knew no bounds. I wanted to return her kindness to the world, to give back rather than give up. Judy embodied kindness. She was love while she lived, and was returned to love in death. Her spirit would live on in every act of love and kindness we committed.

INTRODUCTION — CHRIS

Erik, Brad, and I grew up together playing high school rugby in Powell River, a small coastal mill town, five hours north of Vancouver. We attended university together in Victoria and for four years we held tight to our friendship through rugby scrums, late-night road trips, and many, many term papers. Like most starving students, we worked nights at restaurants looking for a free meal and money for the month's rent. That's where I met Val. Although our academic backgrounds differed (Val was an English Literature major and I was in geography), we discovered a mutual interest in pursuing careers in media. We were both committed to the goal of using television to improve lives. With Erik we began to define a vision that would eventually allow us to change the world through kindness. Brad was there to share the dream and, after taking care of his ailing mother for two years, he was ready to join the team.

At the time, "reality television" was just beginning to grow in popularity, but after witnessing the distorted reality presented in these series, we were even more inspired to develop a show that *dis*couraged conflict ("if it bleeds it leads") and was grounded in social change. We believed we could create television that inspired and informed while entertaining; television that focused on solutions rather than problems; television that empowered people by giving them tools to change their lives.

Together, we strived to develop a "reality" show based on a group of real friends rather than one contrived for the purpose of building drama and conflict. We wanted to create an opportunity for audiences to witness real people who wanted to make a difference in the world and who were doing it in fresh, entertaining ways. With a hand-held camera we began to shoot an Internet Web show with the express purpose of helping others to "seize the day." It featured four segments, the first, "Urban Active Extreme," offered urban adventures to parking police, stockbrokers, and anyone willing to be kidnapped from work to play tennis or head into the heart of the city for skateboarding lessons. All participants embraced our guerilla filmmaking and people marvelled at the release of breaking away from the norm.

In the segment "Top 100 Experiences," we helped people realize one thing they dreamed of doing in the course of their lifetimes. Cameras rolling, we interviewed a taxi driver who had always wanted to eat peanuts at a Yankees game, a child who wanted to ride an elephant bareback, and a university student who wanted to travel to Everest's base camp. With our $500 camera and 50¢ budget we couldn't help too many financially, but we were hopeful that our own dream of having a television show would be fulfilled and perhaps then we could make a few of theirs come true. Our Web site was soon inundated with requests from dreamers who shared their stories with other like-minded Internet adventurers from around the world.

During the segment "Random Travels," we dug into our shallow pockets and with $500 travelled on the cheap to Mexico to prove that adventure could be completely spontaneous and low-cost. With the cheapest flight coming in just over $400, we would each have less than $100 to survive the week. While travelling in Mexico we experienced the kindness of strangers as locals sheltered us from torrential downpours under their tin roofs, or helped us navigate the jigsawed streets.

On one of the last days in Mexico, after a knee-buckling ride up the Pacific coast to the small village of Yelapa, Erik, in his broken Portu-Spanish (30 per cent Portuguese from his time spent in Brazil and 5 per cent Spanish), tried connecting with the locals under the sun-shaded roofs of a café. When he saw bricks being tossed from the hull of a wooden fishing boat sitting in a foot of water, Erik volunteered us for a couple of hours of back-breaking labour. (The locals were building a school and needed help stacking the bricks into piles on the beach.) Erik's misadventures almost always involved something physically extreme and often painful. He stood on the gunnels of the boat and hurled bricks while Val added each brick to a growing block. We bellowed rugby songs that announced for the first time that we were the Kindness Crew. The locals couldn't help but laugh at the "gringos" who would rather sling bricks than Coronas and they cheered us as the last brick was added. There was little conversation between the fifteen villagers gathered and ourselves, but there was a strong sense of connection and comfort that came from knowing we had given without the expectation of anything in return. Through this simple act of kindness we were able to transcend the cultural and language barriers — kindness was a universal language. This experience helped shape the final segment of our Web show, "Random Acts of Kindness."

We helped wherever help was needed. We cleaned homes, washed dishes, gave yoga lessons on lawns or city streets, and started a free taxi service. Performing random acts of kindness proved to be the most entertaining for all of us — and reactions were always extreme: from elation to frustration, from bafflement (your gifts are free?) to suspicion (there must be a catch to this!). The footage was candid and often hilarious. We quickly coined the phrase "Extreme Kindness" to convey to our audience that kindness could be a daring adventure. In order to hook the next generation of do-gooders, we needed to put a radical spin on something that was too often deemed mundane. For us, kindness was just the opposite: it was outrageous, spontaneous, and unpredictable!

On September 11th, 2001, after a summer of filming, Erik got a call from his roommate's father, a retired history professor. "Turn on the television, World War III has started! I'm not joking!" he said to Erik, his voice trembling. We sat, stunned, in front of the television all day, watching in

Kindness just got cool.

horror as the terrorist attacks unfolded. Like so many others across the continent, we felt helpless. Would people continue to embrace the kindness of strangers in the aftermath of September 11th?

The next day, the four us sat on Brad's deck, reflecting on the paper's shocking headlines: ALL FLIGHTS WORLD-WIDE GROUNDED. THE PENTAGON IN FLAMES. WORLD TRADE CENTER COLLAPSES. The world appeared ready to split at the seams. Having watched the attacks from our living rooms as they happened thousands of miles away, we wondered how anything we did in Victoria could make a difference in New York. Suddenly it occurred to us that perhaps the only thing powerful enough to combat the massive wave of fear and violence sweeping the globe was an equally positive wave of love and kindness.

It was simple really: if we could change the life of just one person and that person in turn changed the life of another, we could start a chain reaction. We would help people to "think globally and act locally," inspiring them to commit small acts of kindness and reminding them of the power they still had to make change in their communities and the world. We had found our mission: to connect the world through kindness!

Erik was ready to go the next day, but Brad (grabbing him by the wrists) explained the need for proper planning before we headed out the door. If we wanted to connect the world through kindness we would need a strategy. Would we fly to every state, province, and territory in North America and spend 24 hours performing random acts of kindness? That plan would help to restore the public's faith in flying, but implimenting it was a logistical and financial nightmare; a three-month driving tour across the continent was the next best thing.

After scouring the Internet for help, we received a reply from a woman named Karen working in a public relations firm in New Jersey saying, "I just love what you boys are doing! How can I help?" She was an expert in "splash media" stories, that is, turning a story into an overnight sensation, a front-page phenomenon. Our story fit perfectly — four college kids who would do anything to help.

Karen got the article featured on American newswire: CANADIAN COLLEGE BOYS KILL AMERICANS WITH KINDNESS. It hit a nerve — Canadian kids who care more for compassion than binge drinking and parties? A cover story about kindness?

As the news blasted from radios everywhere we received a flurry of requests for interviews, including a call from *The Tonight Show* saying they'd love to have us on the next time we were south of the border. From

Tennessee to Texas we hit the airwaves, hoping to inspire Americans with our message of kindness and build momentum for a tour. For the next three months, the story continued to circle, each week climbing higher on the news ladder until it finally jumped back across the border into Canada. Arthur Black of CBC's Radio's *Basic Black* decided to do a feature on four young men from Victoria planning a trip across America to perform random acts of kindness. The news gained ground in Canada as news reporters, intrigued by the stereotype-bashing story of college kids on a road trip visiting senior citizen homes and giving out flowers, gave it full coverage.

In between interviews we worked restaurant jobs to make rent and finance the tour. We also combed the corporate community in our hometown and beyond, looking for socially responsible businesses that saw value in raising awareness and supporting our mission. Jeff Timmins of Columbia Sportswear was one of the first to come aboard, offering merchandise to clothe ourselves and others along the way. Stastical Anylsis Software (SAS) provided us with financial support and Sole Custom Footbeads also became a sponsor.

The logistics of the tour meant many phone calls and emails to organize acts of kindness in combination with non-profit organizations that needed our help. In every major centre we organized a Kindness Marathon during which, from dawn to dusk, we hit the streets to perform as many acts of kindness as possible. If a roof needed fixing we'd help. If a teacher wanted us to speak at her school, we'd be there. If a house needed cleaning, we'd scrub it from top to bottom. The tour featured kindness 24/7.

The summer approached, six months past our proposed starting date of January 1st, 2002. Unfortunately, we hadn't raised enough money to venture across the whole continent; given our limited funds we would have to cut the United States from the tour. We felt deflated by our inability to get the project off the ground, but though we were down we were not out.

Meanwhile, in Victoria, we continued Random Kindness Thursdays, testing the marathon concept on our local citizens. In a converted 1960s ambulance, known as the Kindness Cruiser, we staked out storefronts, preying on pedestrians in the hope of making their day with offers of a glass of freshly squeezed lemonade; babysitting services; a crew to scrub pots and pans; free parking (plugging the meters until the coffers dried up); manning the desk while secretaries absconded from work to enjoy a free fruit salad.

Then, suddenly, it all started to fall into place. In the course of a conversation one night after hours of planning and wondering when the waiting game would end, we decided to commit 100 per cent to leaving at the end of August — no holds barred. Even if we had to hitchhike we were going! We were motivated by a sense of urgency — it was now or never!

Mid-summer, a pivotal piece of the puzzle materialized. A woman in Ottawa happened to turn on the television to watch a rerun of *Vicki Gabereau* featuring the Extreme Kindness Crew. She thought our proposed tour was a perfect fit for the company she worked for, CHIP

(Canadian Hotel Income Properties) Hospitality. The hotel management firm was guided by strong values and a commitment to community; it was known as the "Hotel with Heart." Their public relations team at head office in Vancouver contacted us to see if we would be interested in their sponsorship. It was a perfect fit. These hotels became Kindness Headquarters across the country, their employees would join in our Kindness Marathons, and both the community and the company would benefit.

To help us with this grand undertaking we assembled a team. David Crow, a friend and fellow student at the University of Victoria, was coaxed into documenting the tour in writing, leaving behind a near-finished degree, a girlfriend, and a planned tripped with his mother to England. Kelly Seaman, a mutual friend, left his newly formed production company with the hope of capturing every kind moment for a documentary film. Dan Cox, a film student and friend of the group, would join us for the first two weeks of the tour to ensure that the launch was filmed perfectly. Jonathon, my brother, abandoned his last year of university to help manage and organize the logistics of the tour. Lorraine Wilson, a publicist from James Hoggan and Associates, one of the premier public relations firms in Vancouver, offered free counsel and served as PR coordinator from the West Coast home base. She took over for Karen. During the three-month tour, Lorraine spent hours managing requests from the media and served as surrogate mother on tour. Her selfless dedication to the project proved pivotal in helping to assure that our message reached the masses.

Chris, Val, Brad, and Erik, ready to hit the road.

With only two weeks to go, the Canadian Extreme Kindness tour was still seriously crippled — we had no wheels! How would 7 crew members, 2 cameras, 3 laptops, and 200 pounds of gear make it across the country? Dreading another year of inaction, we surveyed our options: Greyhound bus, hitchhiking, bicycle. With only two days to go, Vancouver entrepreneur Mike Baker, C.E.O. of Sole Custom Footbeads, offered us a motor-home, shrink-wrapped with enough Extreme Kindness decals to leave nothing to chance. The night before the Extreme Kindness Tour kicked off, Mike rolled into the driveway. Jaws dropped. Thirty-four feet of luxury liner awaited. We piled in, relieved to know that, regardless of our financial constraints, we were going to be able to cross the country — even if we had to coast home!

The final piece to fall into place was our Web site,

essential for spreading the word, but in the days leading up to the tour our host company went bankrupt, causing our site to crash. We worried that Canada would not be able to keep tabs on a tour (touted as an interactive Web show.) Val and I had one chance to convince two corporations of the value of our tour, and then that the work could be completed in the next 24 hours. We were elated when both Radiant Communications, a Web site host, and Net Genetix, a Web site development firm, came on board, saving us from certain disaster.

On August 26th, 2002, the Extreme Kindness Tour kicked off and we embarked on a journey that would take us through every extreme of culture, landscape, weather, emotion, and friendship. For most of us, the tour meant an end to the mundane chores associated with working for minimum wage and the beginning of a journey that embrace the extreme. We were about to radically alter our understanding of Canada, kindness, and friendship. From Victoria, British Columbia, to St. John's, Newfoundland, we would spend three months in close quarters, returning just in time for Christmas.

We hope that the Extreme Kindness Tour inspires and challenges you to *be* the change you wish to see in the world. If you want a better world, start right now! Don't waste a second. Walk into the next room and compliment someone, tell your family that you love them, buy a flower for a co-worker, volunteer in a soup kitchen or a homeless shelter, or visit someone in a hospice. Be kind to yourself, too, and have fun! We hope that you will find, as we did, that only in giving do we truly receive.

Join the Kindness Crew

1. Get together once a week or once a month with family, friends, or co-workers to log on to www.extremekindness.com. Using the Web site as a resource for ideas, become a part of the Kindness Crew by putting your plan into action.

2. Post your story on our Web site and become a part of the kindness legacy. Send us pictures or video clips. Help us show the world that kindness is alive and well. Your adventure might even be chosen to be a part of the next book.

3. Stay connected with other Kindness Crews across the world through our Web site and free monthly newsletter that will headline inspiring stories from across the globe.

BRITISH COLUMBIA

That best portion of a good man's life,
his little, nameless, unremembered
acts of kindness and of love.
— William Wordsworth

VICTORIA — VAL Despite crossed fingers there will be no tickertape parade, no evening news sendoff as the Extreme Kindness Crew leaves Victoria for the ferry and beyond. We had hoped for a crowd of friends and family, raucous cheering, confetti at the curb, hugging marathons, maybe even a few tears, but there's no time for that. There are exactly one million things to do.

In my parents' home, a makeshift mission-control, there are extra phones jacked into the walls, laptops as hot as grilled cheese sandwiches, and three months worth of gear stashed in every available corner. It's a wonder no one has wrapped police crime scene tape around the perimeter. It's a *House & Home* design disaster. My parents, Michael and Grania, have been relegated to the bedroom, but they thankfully come out to cook the odd meal for their soon-to-be-A.W.O.L. son and his best friends. The real issue is, who will mow the lawn while I'm gone?

Chris' parents have made the trip down from Powell River to say goodbye. Erik's family said their weepy farewells a few days earlier and Brad's sister Devon had also said her goodbyes. We sit in the garden sipping iced tea and taking a minute to forecast what the next 100 days will look like. There's an affectionate mix of bewilderment and admiration on my parents' faces. Will their son really be on the evening news massaging the backs of strangers?

"What about *my* massage?" Mom jokes.

Every few minutes I glance nervously at my watch. Mike Baker, one of our sponsors, should be here any minute with the motorhome. He's incredibly late. But after another pitcher of iced tea we hear the blare of an annoying horn. Mike reaches the bottom of the driveway but has second thoughts — the motorhome is too long and can't make the turn — so he parks it in the middle of my street and hops out. Larger-than-life images of ourselves stare back at us thanks to Mike's talented graphics department. Our home-sweet-home on wheels has arrived.

The next few hours are a blur. Chris' parents embrace us all and wish us the best. Erik and I begin to pack the motorhome as Chris runs out for a badly needed haircut and Brad composes a speech for the first press conference in Vancouver. Erik and I cram hockey sticks and pads, a Coleman stove, hundreds of granola bars, skateboards, cameras, yoga mats, and clothes into every nook and cranny. By midnight my parents' house looks normal again and the motorhome looks like it will bottom out the moment it moves.

That night none of us sleep, our heads are filled with soaring aerial views of the Rockies, fields of wheat, the Great Lakes, the soft sandy beaches of New Brunswick.

The next day I hug my parents goodbye like I'll only be gone for the day and tell them I'll see them soon. Dad holds on, laughing, feeling my desire to get going. We catch the first ferry to Vancouver. The day is flawlessly sunny — a banner day, a red cheek day.

VANCOUVER — VAL

The alarm goes off at 4:00 a.m. but Chris and I aren't sleeping. I have been grinding my teeth since midnight. My speech for the press conference has been looping itself in my head all night and we are due at the CBC in 15 minutes for a national interview. I feel like a kid on Christmas Eve. It is day one and already we are stressed. We are on the brink of three months of non-stop kindness across a sprawling country. There are seven of us in a motorhome whose manual recommends no more than two use it for extended journeys, and our tour budget still lacks gas and food money for anything past Calgary — we have yet to negotiate another cash infusion from SAS Canada, our sponsor, to ensure we'll catch a glimpse of the Atlantic. Have we gnawed off more than we can chew?

Absolutely, and that's the way we like it.

Chris and I begin to assemble our outfits/uniforms: crisp red Kindness Crew T-shirts, shorts (pants when it starts to snow), and sneakers. This is our Superman ensemble, the Can-I-help-you? get-up that has people coming up to us every hour saying, "Hey, I saw you guys on the news. You know, I have a friend who needs some help. . . ."

We go over the points we want to address during the interview.

"Val, remind me to say hi to my mom," Chris says.

"Let's say we wanna cook the Prime Misister a pancake breakfast."

We slip effortlessly through the pre-sunrise silence of the downtown core in a cab. Cappuccino machines are still hours away from their first shot of the day and stacks of unread papers sit on every other corner.

At the CBC, that last sacred bastion of all that is Canadian, we sprint up the steps to the security guard, who greets us with a, "Woah, what's the big rush guys? Do you have an appointment?"

"We're here to do an interview with . . ." Chris starts.

"Kindness Crew, right?" We nod. "Yeah, just go through those glass doors, take the elevator to the fifth, follow the signs."

The room rigged for the interview is flooded with light, a little too much light for 4:00 a.m. The interviewer is in Toronto — and a more civilized time zone. After a few audible gulps of coffee, a cameraman comes over and walks us through what will happen.

"You're going to hear the host's voice in the earpiece in about five minutes. When she speaks to you just look at the camera like you're looking at her." Sounded easy.

Despite the relative emptiness of the room — one camera, two chairs, and three bodies — I am suddenly acutely aware there will be millions of eyes on the other side of the lens in a few moments. My heart begins to flutter. I close my eyes and am silently grateful for the fact that our mission can be articulated in six words: to connect the world through kindness.

"Let's have fun, brother," Chris says, patting me on the back. Chris dispels all my anxiety with one moment of contact. I feel a surge of confidence — I'm having the time of my life.

The intro music fades and a slick voice announces, "And with us this morning are two members of the Kindness Crew. Remember their faces Canada, they might be offering you a massage in the next three months. Good morning Kindness Crew! Did our guys in Vancouver get you two some coffee? It's about 4:20 a.m. for you, isn't it? What a huge project to undertake. Tell us about the tour."

Chris and I simultaneously correct our posture and Chris launches into a practised response.

"The Extreme Kindness Tour is a non-profit, three-month gauntlet of goodwill. We'll be cutting wheat in the Prairies and serving soup in Montreal. Companies like CHIP Hospitality, SAS Canada, Itsyoursole.com, and Columbia Sportswear are helping us spread the love, even joining us on the streets."

The voice without a face sounds impressed. "Why are four guys in their 20s doing this instead of launching careers?"

I crack a huge smile and admit, "We're addicted to kindness and want others to experience the same high. People jump into careers too quickly anyway. We're doing what people always say they'll do some distant day in the future, but we're doing it today."

"What do your parents think about all this?"

"They thought we were crazy a few months ago, but now they're watching us on the morning news." Chris and I both mouth, 'Hi Mom.'

"I'm sure they're proud. Good luck and keep us posted."

It wasn't even 5:00 a.m. and already houses from Grand Prairie, Alberta, to Gander, Newfoundland, knew we were coming. We hadn't a clue, but emails were streaming in from across the country. Not a bad day's work before breakfast.

A press conference is scheduled for 10:00 a.m. and it is beginning to look like it might be standing room only. Friends and family, sponsors, members of the media, Lorraine, our publicist, and even a few sports celebrities from the B.C. Lions are tucking themselves into the crowd. Erik's uncle and cousins are giving us the thumbs up every time they think one of us is looking their way. Minaz Abji, the president of CHIP hotels, is about to introduce us.

The French CBC, CHUM television, BCTV, the *Globe and Mail*, the *Province*, and a few independent reporters poise pens above notepads and dust lenses, hoping to catch something worthy of the evening news. The head table is rigged with microphones and name cards so the press can address us individually. Silver water decanters stand at the ready, dripping with condensation, and a giant video screen looms behind the table. My three best friends and I are about to make known our intention to hug strangers for three months straight, or at least until our shoulders dislocate.

But first we have to warm up the crowd. Not five minutes into the press conference, Chris has everyone up on their feet massaging their neighbour to "Flight of the Valkyries."

"We want people to experience the joy of being kind, so it has to start right now!" As Chris says this he wanders over to Minaz and gently starts chopping his neck muscles like a professional masseur. The network cameramen detach their equipment from their tripods and run over to get a close up. Now it's time for the third degree.

The first question comes flying out of the crowd: "Why *extreme* kindness, guys?"

I love this question. "Because the very pairing of the two words is unusual and ignites curiosity. We're trying to breathe new life into volunteerism — a word that makes most people roll their eyes. Kindness *is* an extreme adventure and we hope to hook the next generation of do-gooders and show them that giving back can be outrageously fun."

"What if someone doesn't want your kindness? What if someone refuses a hug?" a lighthearted cynic asks above the eye-line of a feeding frenzy of cameras. There are a few giggles.

Brad picks up the humour in the reporter's voice, but treats the question seriously, at first.

"You have to respect people's boundaries; you've got to be able to read them. A hug is perfect in some cases, but in others the greatest act of kindness is to do or say nothing." Brad continues, trying to look stern. "Our research has shown that smiles are universally well received, though. I've never seen anyone refuse a smile!" Every reporter in the house is scribbling.

"How will you judge whether the tour is successful or not?" a woman asks.

"We're doing that in a number of ways," answers Erik. "The Web site will track visitors and we hope people will come and post their stories on the message board. Another indicator for us will be the media coverage, in Canada and beyond. We've said our goal is to connect the world through kindness. The tour's success will also be a function of how far that message has travelled. So I guess a big part of the tour's success lies in your hands." Erik smiles at the reporters and cameras, clearly pleased with his answer.

The media's appetite appears satisfied for now and it's time to hit the streets and unleash some curbside compassion. We start in front of the hotel with muffins and coffee for cab drivers, those stoic couriers of crusty commuters, rush-hour yogis who twist and turn through raging traffic. When was the last time they got thanked?

Former Canadian football star Louis Passaglia and a

bevy of strong-armed quarterbacks from the B.C. Lions line both sides of the street ready to launch high-speed surface-to-air muffins. With uncanny precision they hurl, hut, and hike pastries inside moving cars. Drivers, recognizing their local heroes, beg for a snack "to go" as the Lions call plays. Louis looks like he is thinking about punting a few. Cab drivers aren't the only ones playing wide receiver. Exhausted moms are snagging passes, couriers are biking with no hands so they can intercept the odd Hail Mary, and urban hikers are taking hand-offs. The morning coffee break has been redefined and "running out to grab a snack" has new meaning.

The next stop is a construction site a few blocks from the hotel. We carry balloons and coolers full of iced tea and peanut butter sandwiches over our shoulders, strutting to a Village People soundtrack only we can hear. The second the workers see food they drop their noisy tools; it is like turning on a television in a room full of screaming children. Lunch is a hit; peanut-buttery conversations are being had by all and sticky, stiff mouths are loosened with iced tea.

Only one worker has not yet crumbled in the face of compassion and Brad can smell it like a shark smells blood. Brad approaches, a trainer assuring a trapped animal. This man will have to hug Brad to claim the iced tea. Brad's target raises his arms above his head, turns his head slowly to the side and sniffs his armpit. He nods; he is ready for his hug. Laughter fills the building and workers buzz their skill-saws and drills in approval. The two embrace and the iced tea is handed over. Brad — outmanoeuvred and outplayed — walks by me muttering something about a book and a cover that can't be trusted. For the CBC cameras, the image of one burly worker standing with a fistful of pink and yellow helium balloons sums up the visit perfectly.

That afternoon we launch a new weapon, a Kindness Protest, a different breed of demonstration altogether. We pick a busy Vancouver street corner and let her fly. Will serial shoppers on Robson open their hearts or will we get crushed under a stampede of stilettos? I change from flip-flops to sneakers. With 20 colourful sheets of cardboard stapled to hockey sticks we set up camp. People are out in droves and the sun is blistering hot. Dripping ice cream cones paint abstract art on the sidewalk. Erik, Chris, Brad, and I each take a corner of the intersection and start yelling at the top of our lungs.

"Who wants to change the world?" Erik bellows. People look at the signs and start to giggle. But, as scientists have observed, in large groups people's collective IQ rises; the afternoon strollers know what is up.

A woman approaches me and says, "I want the one that says YOU'RE HAVING A FABULOUS HAIR DAY!"

"Absolutely. Just pass it off to Brad on the other side." Just three lights have changed since we arrived and our crew has practically blocked off one of the busiest intersections in Vancouver.

As serendipity would have it, Canadian word-wonder and MuchMusic icon Moka Only stumbles across our scene, grabs a sign that says, DON'T FORGET TO CALL YOUR MOTHER! and busts loose.

Kindness Protest jams Vancouver's city streets.

"Take time to be kind and rewind the video," raps Moka for the camera, pulling dreadlocks away from his face. "I never thought I'd be rhymin' 'bout kindness. What's this about again?" He is out for a mellow afternoon stroll, baggy white shirt wafting in the wind and knitted cap pulled down over his dreads, almost seven feet tall and ready to join the fun.

I let the tour T-shirt speak for itself as he reads the back.

"KINDNESS 24/7. That's dope. That's fresh," he says.

"You just walked into our Kindness Protest. We occupy four corners of an intersection, people choose a sign while the light is red, then walk the signs across the street, hooting and hollering, and drop them off on the other side. The world's shortest and nicest demonstration!" Moka seems impressed but is soon mobbed by a pack of female fans who want him to sign autographs.

I grab a sign from the hands of a giddy woman from Texas, who says, "Where's ma huuuug, sweetie?" in a perfect Texan twang. I look at the space between my open arms as her husband takes a picture.

I can hear Chris across the street, yelling at the top of his lungs like a town crier, "Embrace each other. Hug each other!" Cars are laying on horns to oblige signs that say, HONK FOR KINDNESS. A tourist from Mexico is on top of a garbage can clapping and yelling "Bravo! *Belissimo!* Bravo! Bravo!" Young Asian tourists, all wearing identical backpacks, stand taking pictures and helping Brad dispense signs. Two local teenagers have been with us for over half an hour and are passionately enlisting passersby. One car even makes a point of going around the block several times just so its passengers can keep yelling and honking.

Chris is infecting even the most serious of commuters. "You feel the kindness? It just changed your life," he yells to a man in a suit crossing the street. The man does a 360 and reads the sign: EMAIL ME . . . I'LL SCRUB YOUR TOILET!

Our cheeks are burnt; we've been in the sun for hours converting pedestrians to our cause. The protest has given us all a natural high. The public's response has surprised us and we feel like we've given a dose of kindness to the city of Vancouver. With memories of stunned but hysterical protesters carrying our signs, we pack up and head back to the hotel for a well-earned meal and maybe even a bit of sleep.

Will Canada embrace kindness of strangers?

Four young men from Victoria aim to take spontaneous goodwill from coast to coast

BY ALEXANDRA GILL, VANCOUVER

The next day at the breakfast buffet I pile my plate with melon and grab a few papers to scan for coverage, vaguely thinking we'll be lucky to be in one of them.

At my table, I open the front page of the *Globe and Mail* and almost choke on my watermelon. On A3 is a long article and picture of us unloading a truck full of mattresses for the Salvation Army. Melon juice drips onto the newsprint as I read: "Will Canada embrace kindness of strangers?" Yesterday we visited a local shelter and helped off-load over 100 mattresses for the needy on Vancouver's east side. The picture was of Brad, Erik, and me hefting single beds out of a semi and it was on the inside page of Canada's biggest newspaper. The *Vancouver Sun* and the *Province* have covered the tour, too.

Chris wanders into the cafeteria and sees me gasping for air. He snatches up three copies of the *Globe* and speed walks to my table. Slapping them down he opens the first one — all I say is, "Dude, A3." He finds the article, but instead of reading it he moves to the second copy, then the third, like he suspects it's a printing error.

As we get into the motorhome parked in front of the hotel, happily celebrating kindness' overnight fame, we notice our $700 driver's-side mirror is completely ripped off, sideswiped by some careless road-rager. We are crestfallen. The mirror is vital; a city like Vancouver can't be navigated without it. Prepared to delay our departure, we head back to the lobby to ask for directions to a garage.

A woman comes running toward us waving a piece of paper. "We just received a call from the police!" she yells before she has reached us. "Apparently, another driver saw a truck tear your mirror off. The witness saw your Extreme Kindness logo and tailed the truck 'til she got the license plate, then phoned it in. The police have pressed charges, insurance is covering repairs, and we took the liberty of setting up an appointment at the body shop."

While we were busy helping others, others were busy helping us. What goes around, comes around — and fast. As we pull onto the Trans-Canada several hours later, we look into the new mirror and see that above the city, hanging off the crane at the job site we visited yesterday, are the foreman's pink and yellow balloons.

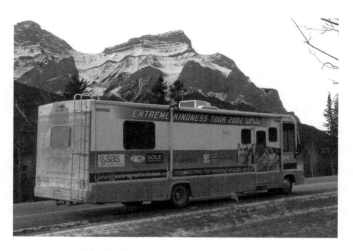

The Kindness cruiser deep in the BC Interior.

MERRITT — VAL

"Welcome rodeo fans!" belts Brad as he reads a freshly painted sign leaning against a wall, shaking like a bullpen. The wall belongs to The Grand and The Grand belongs to Merritt, British Columbia. We are fresh out of Vancouver and this is officially our first stop of the tour. It is 1:30 a.m. and a busload of pretty boys has just stumbled into the heart of Canada's rodeo country. We are about to socialize with folk who wear spurs and all we have to protect us is Brad, our trusty guide.

Brad Stokes is a prairie boy. Raised for a time in the high plains of Hythe, Alberta, Brad rarely goes a day without waxing redneck. Whether it's heroic accounts of tracking gophers at the age of five or waking up at the crack of dawn to milk the cows just so he can eat his

Shreddies, the rest of us can't help but crack an affectionate smile as he regales us with his rawhide-filled reveries. According to Brad's account of his childhood, steaks were as thick as encyclopedias and a crow named Seymour was his best friend. He is a slim, uncallused, blond Marlboro man *sans* cigarettes. When conversation turns to line dancing Brad is the self-appointed master of ceremonies. Given our tour mandate to connect with families in each location, Brad's mission is simple: he has to find a family who will invite us back to their home (preferably farm, ideally ranch) and we'll earn our keep doing whatever chores are required. Brad straight-arms open both doors of The Grand, swaggers in and is swallowed whole. He is wearing a skin-tight tank top, something more for the catwalk than the local saloon.

"Boy'll get tossed out of that bar faster than he'd be tossed off a mechanical bull," Kelly delights, while madly gathering movie equipment. Kelly has ESP when it comes to situations like this.

The Grand is chock-a-block with locals and the air is laced with cigarette smoke, warm Budweiser, and mashed woodchips. Empties and spare change carpet the floor. One-armed bandits line the wall, flashing their dazzling lights to the house band's unusual mix of country covers, Van Morrison, Neil Young, and Cher. The collective twinkling of gold teeth is enough to rival any disco ball. Seven city slickers have just crashed the party and are sizing up the joint.

Brad's look is popular with the ladies and he begins to market himself with some success. Chris has slipped on a purple and pink satin cowboy shirt and rides through the double doors on his trusty steed, a stuffed horse named Eddie. Chris and his horse make friends easily. Eddie is in a chatty mood and if you squeeze his right hoof he will whinny and snort. Kelly is our *paparazzo*, cameras hanging off him like ammunition. He notes everything except the cast. Lighting? Background? Ambient noise? I come in wearing a bright yellow Kindness Crew T-shirt.

Len and Juanita, a young First Nations couple, nearly decline Chris' offer to take Eddie for a ride, and howl, "Muh horse'd be jealous!" but finally consent to take him for a gallop around the pool table. Len pushes up his black cowboy hat with the neck of his Budweiser and says, "I'll give ya'll 10 beer nuts for it."

Len and Juanita have lots of work on their ranch, so we pile into the motorhome like coins into a jukebox and Brad tunes in to the mellow croon of Garth Brooks. We trust he will find us somewhere suitable to spend the night, whether it is taking up 10 parking spaces at the local mall or wedged between dumpsters, clogging an urban side street.

The next morning Chris props himself up on an elbow and rubs a little circle in the motorhome's foggy window. He asks where we are and Brad deadpans, "Followed Len." Brad is a man of few words at the crack of dawn.

The Kindness Cruiser is parked smack dab in the middle of suburbia. Rolling fields filled with frolicking Mustangs are sadly lacking. Instead, precisely manicured lime-green lawns line asphalt perfection. In lieu of horses, tricycles and Nerf footballs speckle the scene. Chris notes that the grass looks well watered and soft, inviting. He promptly grabs his yoga mat, steps outside, finds a nice plot, and begins twisting into a "downward facing dog." In the space of five minutes all members of the Crew are doing sun salutations.

Len appears squinty-eyed mid–yoga session holding a cup of steaming coffee. Wearing only a pair of Wrangler blue jeans and a gigantic smile, he inquires, "Are y'all dancing or what? My neighbours are gunna call the police. You look like yer trying to smell yer feet." He invites us inside to share a cup of coffee and take showers. Passing through the rooms of his house, he crouches down and introduces us to the apple of his eye: his newborn daughter.

He explains an annual summer gathering is taking place at his ranch that evening. Members of his extended family and his band will be there and, if we are sticking around, we will be the guests of honour.

Within 10 minutes Len is fully dressed, twirling his keys as he walks toward his pickup. Following the rising dust cloud behind Len's V8 we head down a long, dusty two-track road. The window of his truck winds down and Len raises his arm, extending his index finger and drawing wide circles in the air. A gesture we interpret as, "Everything you see belongs to me." We bounce down a hill then skid to a stop. Hills and fields ripple with heat, occasional rogue breezes bring temporary relief, smoothing and spiking the sun-bleached wheatgrass,

Erik hauling a driver in Merritt.

creating the illusion of a shivering landscape. It is late August and the land is tinder dry and lifeless.

Len removes the tarp covering the cargo in his flatbed: fence posts. They look like a newly opened box of toothpicks. What are we going to "drive" them with? I don't see any machinery, no heavy equipment, no hammers, no shovels. Len drops an iron pile driver on the ground — imagine a large hollow cigar with two handles off the sides like wings.

If it's an art driving seven-foot posts into holes in dry, sun-scorched earth with a pile driver, then it is a fine art driving posts into ground without holes. Erik balances the driver across his shoulders; he is determined to be the one to pound the first post. It takes 30 slams of the driver to bury the first post 1.5 feet.

"You guys are making it look hard," Len teases. After only one post we have exceptional blisters. But who doesn't enjoy seeing the signs of honest labour, feeling the pulpy evidence of hard work? This is noble stuff, I think, winking at Erik.

We suppose we are marking the edge of his property to keep in the Mustangs that can't be too far off, but we ask to be sure.

Len clarifies. "We're building a golf course, so, scatter a bunch around the place. We're doing a mini fundraiser this year, a buck a round. You have to hit the posts with your ball — my kids'll be finding them for months."

Len strides off through the grass in his boots and leaves us to drive the other 17 posts. When he is about 50 feet away, he turns around and yells, "Ya know when I first met you guys last night, I wasn't sure if you were good guys or not." He waves, turns, and keeps walking. We work hard, fuelled by Len's qualified compliment.

A few posts later a friend of Len's and a man we'd met the night before, Willie, makes his way toward us, grass parting gently at his knees. He is First Nations and proud of his roots. A pretty serious looking cowboy, Willie wears black Levis, a black cowboy shirt with abalone buttons, a black hat, and has a sharp, black goatee. He is the kind of guy who can be profound and crass in the same breath. He speaks slowly and deliberately. With Willie, wisdom and nonsense sit close together. He is a living paradox, he figures, both cowboy and Indian.

He invites us to his farm for a ride; Brad and Erik on greenbrokes while Chris and I listen to his stories. His

Chris and Erik horsing around with a greenbroke in cowboy country.

hands swoop and tack, becoming a horse in one tale, a fish in another, bruising the air to make a point.

"With our people the wisdom is kept with the elders. Children learn at school, sure, but they get wisdom from their parents, grandparents, great grandparents. This random act of kindness, as you call it, is special because it is wisdom coming from the younger generation, wisdom flowing the other way. I think elders can learn from youth. Driving posts is not a big thing. It's a little thing. But you'll leave Merritt tonight and do another little thing in the next town and the next town. These little things add up, mean something big, and we have to thank you for that."

Willie's insight is eclipsed only by his genuine gratitude. We thank him for his words and insist that it is he and Len who are teaching *us* and not the other way around.

With the last fence post sturdy in the dry earth, families and friends begin to gather. Barbecues start to smoke. Juanita and friends are setting up tables for food. Giant sockeyes, their heads still on, spit on the grills.

One of Len's cousins uses his fillet knife and taps the fish on the head. "In a couple of minutes I'll cut out the cheeks, tenderest part of the fish, and if you want I'll save the eyes for you." I say I'll stick to Juanita's pasta salad.

Len works the crowd, now 150 strong, telling everyone that the golf course was our handiwork and then summons us to the garage. "I told you we were having a fundraiser right? One of the families here has a daughter who is autistic. We're raising money for her therapy. You helped us raise a couple hundred bucks. We'd like to thank you."

We feel like we are in a story that has already been written. Our fortuitous encounter with Len, the fence posts, Willie's insights, and now this — even though it isn't much, we have had a hand in easing another family's pain. Everything about our stay in Merritt has the rhythm and feel of fate.

Len says that it's a First Nations tradition to bid travellers farewell by singing them a song, especially before a long journey. The song will linger with us and protect us from harm. Eight men carrying drums shaped like giant tambourines surround us. It starts with one voice, wailing, softening, climbing. The singer begins to delicately tap his drum. The other men join, dancing and spinning low to the ground. I can smell the breath of the dancers they're so close. Voices are gaining momentum now and there are yips as the rhythm picks up.

The sun is setting in front of us just as our farewell song ends, unexpectedly, like a phone conversation disconnected. And that is our goodbye. We walk silently toward the purple of the horizon and the next little thing.

SALMON ARM — ERIK

Rolling up the driveway of the Hammer family farm, it feels like we're coming home. The dogs, Maya and Boots, come running out to meet us and Paula, Steve, Blair, and Jesse are waiting on the front step of the house. More than a full year has passed since Paula first invited us to Salmon Arm for an attempt at the random act of kindness Guinness World Record, but if feels like last week. We had spoken at several schools, dug ditches, planted saplings, exercised dogs, picked up garbage — over 18,000 acts of kindness in 12 hours thanks to our fellow Kindness Crew members in the community.

We sprint across the driveway for hugs like soldiers coming home from a tour overseas. Kelly, Dan, and Dave have not met the Hammers, but given the stories we shared I'm sure they feel like they have. The Hammers open their lives and home easily and the support crew is instantly recognized as part of the family. Blair is an effervescent 13 year old with a trusting nature and her 16-year-old brother, Jesse, is a small town ruffian with an open heart and mind. The siblings had pleaded for the afternoon off school in honour of our arrival and they plan to make good use of it. We follow Blair and the smell of cooking garlic into the open kitchen and begin to prepare the evening feast. Jesse takes an ecstatic Kelly and Chris exploring the back 40 on ATVs for a couple of hours before dinner. Val, Dave, and Dan lounge in the living room listening to Steve relate hair-raising Harley Davidson experiences.

Eventually the boys return home with a few of Jessie's friends from down the street in tow. They stomp muddy boots off on the front porch and begin to pile noisily through the front door. Almost simultaneously the kids from Paula's random acts of kindness pack, a youth group committed to spreading kindness in Salmon Arm, begin to show up with their parents in a parade of dusty minivans and trucks. Family friends who had been a part of the world record attempt fill the driveway packing armloads of Tupperware and in no time the house is full. Apparently everyone is staying for dinner.

Homemade spaghetti with rich tomato sauce, crisp Caesar salad, fresh pepperoni pizza, homemade garlic toast — it looks like a full-page spread in *Canadian Living* — for about 10 seconds. Everyone grabs paper plates and ravages the food with a ferociousness normally reserved for the wolves found in woods behind the Hammer farm. The chaotic bustle lasts about 15 minutes before everyone has found a niche where they can sit down and enjoy.

Paula stands up from her stool and calls the crowd to attention.

"Hello? Everyone! I just want to say how lucky we are to have you all here. We are joined by a really special group of guys who have made a big difference in my life and the life of our family. They went out of their way to come here and I want to thank the Kindness Crew for coming home to Salmon Arm."

The house pulses with energy until late into the evening, when someone suggests we tackle the kitchen. There is nothing that clears out a house faster than a large pile of dishes. We clean and laugh and tell the Hammers the kind of things you can't tell anyone but family. One by one we say good night, brush our teeth, and wander out to the motorhome. I crawl up onto my dashboard makeshift bed (seriously) and into my sleeping bag. Looking out the front window I have a perfect view of the night sky. The horizon to the north is layered with the soft dancing shapes of the northern lights and the stars are illuminated with a brilliance only seen in the country. The cold is raw and beautiful and I feel like I'm slipping into Van Gogh's *Starry Night*. Genuine exhaustion pulls at my eyelids and the northern lights flicker to darkness.

The next morning I steal over Dave and Kelly, the morning ogres, trip out the creaky motorhome door, and sprint, yoga mat in hand, toward the sunlit front porch. I roll my mat out on the deck, take a lungful of mountain air, and ease my way into my first sun salute. As I move into Cobra posture I can feel the sun warm my face and neck. Since starting the tour, our time has been scheduled around media events, conference calls, Web site uploads, tour planning. There is no downtime. One minute we are in front of the media, the next minute we are "relaxing" at a social function while being asked to defend our position on kindness. As models for kindness we have to be sensitive to the fact that people are always watching. After several days it becomes very taxing. We have to take our own advice and be kind to ourselves. Today is our first glorious day off — time to eat fresh berry pancakes with cream, relax, and see where the hours take us.

The Hammer kitchen is filled with all the things that distinguish a home from a house. School projects hang on the wall, faded comic strips and dog-eared photos stick to the fridge, and homemade birthday cards fill the windowsill. On the breakfast counter sits a book, in which each morning the Hammers record what they are thankful for. Initially the idea met resistance but by this point it has become a ritual. It is filled with the mundane and magnificent things that make up daily living. From "Mom making me lunch" to "My children's health and happiness," the book is filled with genuine sentiments too true to be left unsaid.

The day is spent leisurely writing, editing, reviewing old footage, riding horses with Paula, offroading with Jessie, running unexplored deer trails with the dogs, and bouncing on the trampoline with Blair. Salmon Arm is heaven.

"C'mon Erik! Put your back into it!" Chris yells, like an ornery deputy working a chain gang. The sun bakes the Neskonlith First Nations reserve. Paula has used her community connections to volunteer us for hard labour in service of the local First Nations band. We are clearing the land in preparation for the Kanoowhen T Wawh Cultural Centre.

Sweat drenches our shirts as we hack at the unending wall of undergrowth. In fact, it should be classified as overgrowth. The cattails, salmon berry plants, and black berries had, in places, reached six feet. I swing wildly at them with a shovel and they fall on me, matting sticks and burrs into my hair. All other Weed Eaters and scythes have been snatched up by the keenest of the 20 volunteers who had joined our crew. I am forced to make do with the remaining tools. Val is strapped into the giant gas-powered Weed Eater and is now surrounded by a yellowish green aura of pollen, spray, and disturbed insects. The scene is surreal. Other tool-deprived volunteers follow behind to load mattress-sized piles of debris onto their backs and haul them out to massive piles on the road. Gradually, the field that had been left fallow for years is being dissected and the tunnels begin to connect. Brad, our allergic worker, is marching the dusty piles of cut grass and pollen-filled cattails out to the road with ant-like diligence. With swollen eyes watering, nose running, he can barely take a breath without sneezing. He has been working in the hot sun for at least two hours and has yet to take a break.

Chris, who has been taking a 45-minute water break and is screaming at me through the tunnel, "for encouragement," has now taken a break from his break for an impromptu telephone interview with the *National Post*. After a few minutes Chris passes off the cell phone to Brad, who marches out of the bush, plops down on an exposed stump, and sneezes through a few questions. Studio interviews are often very sterile, so to convey energy it is often necessary to paint a picture. Modern media has trained audiences to expect unfulfilled promises and over-inflated talk, but when you begin to expose them to something genuine and immediate, the message is that much more powerful. Here, we are so deeply entrenched in "the picture" it is almost overwhelming; we are in "the field," both figuratively and literally.

The cell phone is thrust through the bushes to me. "How does Salmon Arm compare to other places you have been or expect to visit?"

"I can't say enough good things about the people of this town. They represent everything that is good about rural communities."

The reporter has everything she needs so I wrap my blistered and bleeding hands around a shovel and begin swinging it through the foliage toward the sound of the Weed Eater and Val.

We are winning.

Steve raps on the windshield at 5:45 a.m. to drag us to his Rotary meeting. Seeing Steve at his "real job" is a little like being shown the secrets of the universe. Steve is never around in the morning; he vanishes sometime in the night and materializes later in the day to check up on our adventures. It's the way things work, and we accept it. But now that Steve is dressed in a suit and tie, we dismiss images of him roughing up thugs with gambling debts and concede that he is legitimate after all. He has been living a double life: by day he is more like Steve Jobs, a man with a work ethic and a plan. By night he resembles Steve McQueen, a fearless biker and rebel with a cause.

We pile into Steve's truck and head to breakfast with the The Daybreak Club members of the Salmon Arm chapter of Rotary Club International. Naturally, we are called upon to say a few words about the tour. We explain our difficulties planning the tour, share our recent adventures in Merritt, and boast that we plan to carry Salmon Arm's world record challenge to the rest of the country. Salmon Arm has set the benchmark for kindness. The talk is informal as business men and women inquire about logistical and financial aspects of the tour. The president stands up to thank us and presents us with an unexpected cheque to help offset tour expenses. Once again Salmon Arm has come through.

We step out onto sunlight-drenched steps where Paula is waiting to take us to her friend Millie's gym, Curves for Women. Chris jokingly inquires about the possibility of working out at the exclusively women's gym and much to our surprise it has already been arranged. Within 10 minutes we are stripping down in the change room (unfortunately recently emptied for our arrival). After a short demonstration of how the gym works we join the rest of the women for a workout that earns us each a gold star on the wall — something usually reserved for people who have lost weight. After we have worked up a serious sweat, Millie leads us out onto the lawn where she has a picnic brunch waiting.

The last thing Paula has scheduled for us is a community soccer game at a local field. When we arrive it's early evening and the pitch is filled with about 35 men and women and an exciting pre-game energy. There are a few new faces, but most of the players hovering between the lime chalk lines kicking balls back and forth are kids or adults we have spent time with in the last few days.

This is the way people from Salmon Arm tell you you're one of the family: they include you. It's not religious, it's not out of obligation, it's just the way things work in this community. They treat you like you have lived there all your life.

As the whistle blows and cool mountain air fills my lungs I lunge into the action. Due to varying skill levels, at times it looks like World Cup highlights on Soccer Saturday and at others it looks like a Sunday morning Peewee game. When someone finally shouts, "Next goal wins!" Chris squeaks past our virtually impenetrable defence, taps one into the top left corner, and everyone cheers, happy to give their aching legs a rest. The soccer game *is* Salmon Arm: a hard-working, friendly, and diverse group of people who come together to achieve a goal. In the days ahead we will remember these people and realize that we carry the same power to work together as a community.

Hard Labour

1. Organize a crew.
If you are trying to enlist friends to participate in a project that requires hard labour begin with clear, easy-to-follow directions to the location, a schedule and timeline, discussion of the goal you hope to achieve, and the reasons why you're taking this on. Recruit people who have experience in labour-intensive jobs (they can use their expertise to aid your cause and can also put a new spin on an old game) and those who don't (they may have skills in areas you didn't know they had). Tell sceptics that if they don't enjoy themselves they don't have to come out again . . . but encourage them to give it a try once.

2. Access your resources.
Once you have a crew of motivated people at the site at the appropriate time, it's up to you to get things going. You have already done most of the work to make the project happen. The hard work is setting it all up and the rest is fun. In order to get the project rolling it is important to make sure each person is on the same page. When everyone arrives have a "pre-game huddle"

where the logistics are taken care of and everyone knows their task. Make sure everyone has the proper tools and provide food and drink for breaks.

3. Stick to the schedule.

Nothing takes the energy out of a project more than delays. Be honest with everyone. Do not push beyond the goal unless you are sure everyone wants to keep going. When you're done, have a "post-game wrap up." Congratulate everyone and go over the highlights. Head out for a meal or relaxation as a group of friends and bask in the satisfaction of a task well done.

4. Pay it Forward.

Publicize your event. The media loves to fill their "recreation slot" with a feel-good story that involves a crowd and an honourable goal. Call all the media you can think of — radio stations, television stations, newspapers, newsletters, Web sites, and town criers. No medium is too big or too small — every publicity mention you receive creates momentum. When the media does arrive give them something newsworthy. Have everyone dress up in animal costumes to put a new roof on SPCA and you will get coverage. That said, don't be disappointed if no media show up. Don't take it personally; it happens. Ask yourself if this is something you would be interested in. If it is, stay your course, someone will give you coverage.

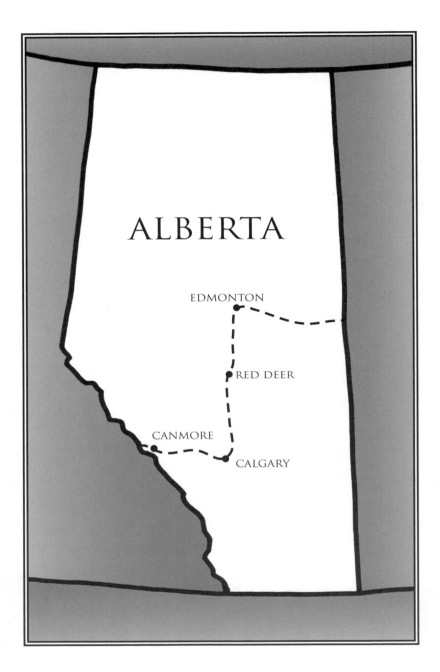

ALBERTA

There is no duty more obligatory than the
repayment of kindness.
— *Cicero*

CANMORE — ERIK
The next morning we negotiate the packed motorhome through the awe-inspiring Rocky Mountains. The highland is calling us onward and upward to Canmore! The stereo crackles to life with smooth rhythmic house beats, a sure indication that Val is at the helm. No matter how many times you make your way through the Rockies they will never cease to amaze. When in their midst you feel a sort of connection to nature that you don't get anywhere else. The road weaves impossibly through the sheer grey faces of granite dwarfing our 34-foot motorhome. It is all we can do to keep the motorhome on the road as we are constantly distracted by mountain sheep, jade green lakes, and rock face.

The Radisson Hotel in Canmore looks over a mountain range offering an unimpeded view of Ha Ling Peak. Ha Ling, with its sheer rock face, is named in memory of several Chinese wives who lost husbands to unsafe working conditions during the construction of the Canadian Pacific Railroad. Overwrought with grief, the women threw themselves off the cliff.

We are greeted by the Radisson kindness team, who brief us on the schedule for the upcoming days and show us to our rooms. Included in the team is Jay, head chef at the Radisson's fine dining restaurant and brother-in-law of long-time Victoria friend, Mark Luttrell. A varsity basketball player and mountaineer, Mark has a heart as big as his shoes and it is soon apparent this also applies to others in his family.

Jay also owns Mountain Bone, an all-natural dog bone company. He presents us with several boxes of bones to hand out to happy dogs across the country. Jay mentions offhandedly that his restaurant, though understaffed, has booked a large European tour group for dinner that evening. As we've all worked as waiters, we jump at the chance to pitch in.

For the rest of the afternoon Chris explores the boardwalks and runs the trails through town, while Dave, Kelly, and Dan begin a pickup game of hockey in the parking lot. Val hits the stationary bike in the gym and I bust out my yoga mat after putting on some laundry. I return to find my clothes missing from the dryer but folded neatly. No note, just a simple random act of kindness. I am grinning from ear to ear.

At 5:00 p.m. we get the lay of the restaurant, are assigned our sections, and assume that what we lack in menu knowledge we can make up for in humour. As the restaurant swells with British guests we schmooze our way through the menu and do our best to entertain. When confronted with late food or a lack of knowledge, the Crew tells stories about the tour and lets the Brits know that a BBC reporter will be joining us on the streets tomorrow.

When all is said and done the restaurant does almost twice its usual business. Bumbling and uneducated we still end up with more than $400 in tips. Everyone at the restaurant is very appreciative of our help and almost ecstatic when Val, ever the altruist, takes all our tips and distributes them among the kitchen staff. None of us feels comfortable keeping the money and we are happy to give it to the people who deserve it the most.

Although we are exhausted and have a big day ahead, we linger in the restaurant sharing stories well into the night. After a trip to the steam room and a late-night hot tub, we collapse into bed.

The next morning, with a caravan of vehicles and hotel employees, we head toward Restwell R.V. Park. We pack each vehicle full of warm baked goods, hot coffee, and cleaning supplies. The mission: to bring a little bit of sunshine to this otherwise cool and rainy morning.

The time is 8:00 a.m. and there is no noticeable sign of life in the neighbourhood, so the Kindness Crew takes the first step and decides to go door-to-door offering refreshments and cleaning services. We wash grimy windows, clean dirt-stained linoleum floors, and scrub week-old dishes left in the sink. A woman from Switzerland, still dazed by the hour and the oddity of our campaign, is so excited she promises to pay it forward once she returns home.

Judy Aldus, the aforementioned reporter for BBC, is taping this Kindness Marathon for a radio documentary to be aired internationally a week later. She follows us from trailer to trailer and begins to understand what we are doing. Most of the time, reporters look at what we're doing on paper and think, "It sounds like a good idea but there must be some sort of catch." When they meet us they usually ask similar questions in an interested, polite, but sceptical tone. It's not until we actually hit the streets together that they begin to realize what we're doing. After a few random acts of kindness an amazing transformation takes place. The reporter begins to realize that not only are there people in the world creating something that is genuinely good, but that they can join in. Judy Aldus makes that journey with us as the morning moves on. Journalists so often report on the worst that happens in the world; our story is news because it is an exception.

While hotel employees scurry back and forth in the rain giving warm muffins and fresh coffee to drivers heading off to work, we offer massages, sing "Happy Birthday" over the phone, and assist an elderly woman with her packing. With each appreciative hug, word of thanks, and smile, a great lesson is reinforced: you can't judge someone's need for kindness by the way they look; *everyone* needs kindness.

Brad raps his cold knuckles on an aluminum door, which squeaks open to reveal a very large man with tribal tattoos and some serious piercings.

"Yes? What can I do for you?" he asks, a stern look on his face.

Brad appears to be recalling the lessons he had learned on how to deal with large bears and dangerous animals: "Do not run away. Make slow and steady movements. Remember they are as afraid of you as you are of them."

"Good morning," he pipes up in a surprisingly clear voice. "We're doing random acts of kindness this morning. Do you have any cleaning that we could do? Or perhaps you'd like a Danish?"

"Really? Thanks, I'd love one. I just got off work. Hey, are you the guys from the paper?"

Brad is beaming. Time after time we are proven wrong when business people, commuters, tourists, and very large tattooed men welcome our kindness with open arms. After a few weeks we are beginning to realize that the people who are often stereotyped as unapproachable are the ones who need kindness most. Occasionally, someone lives up to the stereotype and we get snubbed, but by the end of our brief interactions most are keen to find out if there is anything they can do to help, and have committed to paying it forward.

The sun is beginning to overpower the clouds by the time we leave the park, and we head to the Visitor Information Centre to hand out flowers, feed dogs, and give out snacks to hungry travellers. Before we get started, we relax on damp grass to eat lunch.

"How can we make this interesting and exciting?" is a question we constantly ask ourselves, and today is no exception. To make kindness exciting you have to keep it fresh. We had given out flowers on tens of occasions in Victoria before the tour, so how were we going to make today unique? The answer was: diversify and get creative. Val and I decide to offer the flowers as if we are proposing marriage. Val sticks the flowers in the neck of his T-shirt and invites tourists to choose from his "vase."

Chris offers dog bones to travellers' pooches and we brighten the days of people from Germany, France, the United States, and from virtually every province in Canada. Canmore quickly becomes a metaphor for the kind of exponential change we are hoping to create throughout our tour. It's just a small town nestled in the Rocky Mountains, but through simple random acts of kindness we begin a ripple effect that has the potential to create positive change around the world.

By the time we have spent our supply of flowers, a majority of the hotel staff is exhausted but happy. When participating in any activity where you are dealing with the public for an extended period of time, you have to sustain a high level of energy and restock your resources through moments alone, but Kindness Marathons are different. The first few are exhausting because you are constantly giving, but after a while you tap into a new energy resource. You begin to draw from the positive energy you have created in the lives of the people you interact with. When you first realize this it is akin to the second wind racers talk about while running a marathon, that extra burst of energy that sustains you just long enough to finish.

The first part of our Kindness Marathons involve structured kindness activities, but we generally seek out something unique and unplanned during the second part of the day. So, that afternoon, armed with coolers of fruit and a spirit of adventure, we head into the heart of Canmore. I distribute some of the mountain bones Jay gave us to local puppies. I've got the biscuits wedged in my mouth and have dogs licking and chewing them from between my lips. I am often amazed at the things someone (OK, me!), will do in front of a camera. I believe it's called Kodak courage.

Chris has commandeered Kelly, who is filming his newly invented game: get people to pay the fruit forward. He passes off a bunch of bananas and persuades a random passerby to give away the fruit to people he meets. Brad and Val are working together with our camera and are filming interviews and giveaways with the hotel staff, thus leaving me out of all filming and activity. Dejected, I wipe the drool from my face, give the rest of the package of dog bones to a dog owner, and walk down the street.

"Fine, I don't need a camera to make a difference. I'll just go change the world by myself," I huff. Of course, I realize this is ridiculous. The reason we are here in the first place is because we work together as a team, but I am annoyed just the same.

Random acts of kindness are a great way to explore a

new place. Not only does it provide you with something to do, it also introduces you to people you would never otherwise meet. I wander down the charming sunlit streets alone until I am standing in front of a saloon referred to by locals simply as "The Ho." A girlfriend of mine had worked there and said it was one of the more unusual stops in Canmore. Inside the dark and smoky bar I strike up a conversation with the bartender, then distribute bananas to the local barflies who look like they could use some form of sustenance besides beer and cigarettes. I fall into comfortable conversation with some of them about the virtues of kindness.

"You mean you're travelling across the country just doin' good things for people and yer not getting paid?" exclaims a skinny local in his mid-30s from behind a veil of smoke. He can't quite understand the concept, though he can't find anything particularly wrong with it either. He assumes the tour is a new way to pick up women and it takes me several strained and confusing minutes to convince him first, that I'm not trying to pick up women, and second, that I'm not now trying to pick up him. "Well, I guess so, you seem like an alright guy to me partner — have fun."

I saunter out into the blinding sunshine, sneeze three times, and continue on my tour.

Having given out all my bananas, I am now out of ammunition, but full of ambition. I let my feet lead the way to a natural health food store where I meet a beautiful woman behind the counter who almost proves the barfly's point.

I stumble, "We're going across the country committing random acts of kindness. Is there anything I can do to help?" My voice cracks. Smooth Erik, very smooth.

She looks at me. I *am* wearing a shirt that plainly says KINDNESS CREW on the front, she *has* read about us in the paper, I don't look like a *complete* psychopath, although she hasn't entirely ruled that out.

She admits that she needs strawberries, melons, and bananas from the grocery store to make her store's famous smoothies, and it has been so busy that she hasn't been able to leave to restock. She hands me enough cash for the purchase and before you can say naturopathic healing I am out on the street with a mission, but with absolutely no idea where the nearest grocery store is. After numerous wrong turns, several random acts of kindness, and two unsuccessful forays into grocery stores, I finally find the IGA. I help collect buggies, buy the fruit, and break into a "grocery jog" on the way back to town, realizing that I have been gone for almost an hour and the young woman probably suspects theft.

To the contrary. "That was quick," she says.

"Aaaaaaa, I had to go to two different stores and I managed to do some random acts of kindness on the way," I bumble.

"Well, thank you, that was very helpful. I think what you guys are doing is great."

I blush and then, not being able to think of anything intelligent to say I mumble thanks and shuffle out to find the rest of the Crew.

Suddenly Brad and Val leap out from behind a building.

"How does it feel to be the most sought after man in Canmore?" Brad shouts from behind the camera.

I am stupefied and smiling. "What are you talking about?"

"We've been tailing you Hanson," says Val with a big grin. "Interviewing anyone who you ran into on the streets, anyone you did random acts of kindness for. We also noticed you lingered quite a while in the health food store. What was going on there?"

"Ahhh, nothing. Let's get back to the hotel, we've got work to do."

The crew had noticed I was missing and had headed off on a mission to find me. Even though we work as a team there are times during the tour when each of us becomes disillusioned with the other members' visions. It's always important to reference the positive and realize that sometimes our plans may differ but our intentions are the same. It was a lesson I didn't soon forget. Friends shape your world; respect them, share with them, and trust them.

The credo of the Kindness Marathon is "dawn 'til dusk" so we wearily pick up assorted garden tools and a squeaky wheelbarrow from the hotel and head out in search of dirt. En route we run into a pack of runners picking up race packages for a half marathon the next day. Immediately Chris and I devise a plan to run the race and get out of random gardening for the rest of the evening. We will have our race and run it too. The race director is in desperate need of people to hand out timing chips, small devices strapped to the runners' wrists to electronically record race times. We volunteer the Crew and reason that it's all right to abandon the gardening mission in lieu of the next day's commitment.

Like most long-distance races the CAUSE annual half marathon starts at an hour only runners can survive, so, early in the morning we layer on all the Columbia clothing we have and head up the mountain to the Nordic Centre, the site of the 1988 Winter Olympic Games. After piling out of the warm van into the frigid mountain air, we take our volunteer positions only to discover our trusted race director has thrown us to the dogs! Within an hour, hundreds of spandex-covered bodies shuffle toward us like cattle jostling for position at the morning food trough. Steam is actually rising from the crowd as we frantically try to accommodate everyone waving a pink, green, or orange race number.

Instantly we are transformed from laid-back race volunteers to security guards and human information booths. People are trying to grab their own tags and are asking us questions we have no idea how to answer: "How do these things work?"; "Is this a fast or a slow course?"; "Have you seen my son? He's wearing spandex and a green windbreaker." Chris and I have given out almost 1300 chips in the span of an hour and now leave Brad and Val to join the other runners.

The announcer shouts, "Welcome runners to the 2002 CAUSE 10K and half marathon. The timing chips on your ankles will record your time as soon as you pass through the sensor so please stand back from the start line. I would also like you all to put your hands together for Chris Bratseth and Erik Hanson. This is their first 10K race so please wish them well! Thank you, enjoy the race!"

Applause erupts. Shocked, Chris and I, both seasoned runners, lift our arms in the air, laughing out loud. Val must have gotten to the announcer.

"On your mark . . ."

My heart beat a little faster as a surge of adrenaline hit my bloodstream.

"Get set . . ."

It's amazing how nervous you can get running *for fun*.

BANG! We are off and my legs feel like Jello. Chris and I sprint to the front of the pack and are leading for the first few minutes of the race. Gradually more experienced racers take the lead and we shout words of encouragement to them as they pass. Beneath their breath every single one thanks us as they pump by. Chris and I ease into a comfortable pace intending to have as much fun as possible.

At every junction we jokingly attempt the wrong turn, sending the volunteers first into a panic then into fits of laughter. We cheer the people who sit on their front lawns cheering us and perform acrobatic running manoeuvres over fire hydrants. After 40 minutes and side cramps from running and laughing we head down the final stretch, hand in hand. The race watchers applaud and, ever the crowd pleaser, Chris takes this as a queue to leap, mid-run, onto my back and start smacking my butt like a horse. I piggyback Chris over the finish line and collapse.

Back at the hotel we spend the remainder of the day competing in a street hockey game. Sticks and gear have been donated and everyone from the hotel joins in, including many of the patrons. Jay cooks up a barbecue lunch to feed the growing number of hungry players watching from hotel chairs in the parking lot. From elderly housekeepers to nimble-limbed bellboys, *Hockey Night in Canada* has come to the Radisson.

After dinner we hold a gruelling but necessary team meeting to discuss the kinds of issues that make the tour flow smoothly. The meetings are never planned but usually occur spontaneously during dessert about once a week. We discuss: group dynamics; personal feelings; the next tour stop in Calgary; our lack of finances; and who we would be if we could be one of the main characters from *Star Wars*.

The next day there is no denying the call of the mountains. It is our last day in Canmore and Ha Ling Peak has been beckoning through the giant glass windows in the dining room of the Radisson for our entire stay.

Leaving all the pollution, noise, frustration, and inhibition on the trail behind us, we pass several hikers on the switchbacks who graciously accept our offers of encouragement and energy bars. In return they relay that we have a long way to go and that it's a *lot* steeper than it looks. We secretly laugh in the face of danger. We are young, high on mountain air, and have an excess of energy to burn.

After an hour and a half of hiking, the foliage begins to thin and the trees surrounding the trail become more weathered and gnarled. The trail works itself into a narrow mountain-goat path that climbs up the bare and rocky back of the Ha Ling Peak. We crest the top of the hill and the view explodes beneath us while 30-knot winds assault our warm faces. There, far below, is Canmore and the expansive Bow Valley.

I am on top of the world when Brad smiles and says, "I can't imagine being closer to Mom. It's easy to let go of a lot of trivial stresses when you're up this high and you've got this kind of perspective."

Ha Ling is not just a summit, it's a place where we can reflect on where we've been and where we are headed. We are happy and excited to see what adventures will present themselves in Calgary and beyond.

CALGARY — VAL
The Three Sisters that form Canmore's razor-edged ridge looked like they could slice the heavens open: Canada in 3-D. Now we are entering the pancake portion of the country and have to adjust our vertical expectations to appreciate the horizontal. Cowtown appears on the horizon, home to top sirloin and stampedes.

We are picking up Chris' younger brother, Jonathon,

who will try to manage us for the remaining two and a half months. We need someone to handle the incoming requests and keep us in line. We have been inundated — our cell phones haven't stopped buzzing. The time it takes to field the calls distracts us from executing the acts of kindness we have committed to performing. Jonathon can help sort the requests and free us to focus on giving rather than taking.

Our stop in Calgary coincides with the one-year anniversary of the September 11th tragedy. Since the events in New York had inspired us to strike out and spread kindness, we were looking forward to the opportunity to do something unique to mark the day. Ironically, our phones have been relatively silent heading into Calgary: the September 11th anniversary is understandably the main event for the media and we have received little interest. The tour is naturally a feel-good piece and, we think, balances all the negative news in the headlines, but we'll have to do something worthy of attention. In the home of the Saddledome, life-sized bronze bulls litter street corners, lassos are sold at corner stores, and they aren't going to take us seriously unless we come up with something on a grand scale.

And then we do. On the Stephen Avenue Walkway four guys with 30 large pieces of cardboard, heaps of crayons, felt pens, and pencil crayons are encouraging pedestrians to write love letters to the people of New York. We will send these missives of goodwill to a post office in the Big Apple with instructions to put them in random mailboxes. It is a small but heartfelt gesture and it says what we want to say.

People compose poems, draw pictures, and draft words of support. Ladies in suits kneel on the ground, scuffing their nylons. A man in a wheelchair, unable to write, dictates a message. As a parting gift we give everyone who participated two Post-it Notes with reminders that YOU CAN'T BUY LOVE, GIVE IT AWAY! and TODAY IS THE BEST DAY OF MY LIFE, BUT TOMORROW WILL BE EVEN BETTER! One of these human bumper stickers is for the person who wrote the card and the other is to pass on. We give away hundreds.

EDITOR: JOHN GRADON 235-7569   CANADA.COM/CALGARY/CALGARYHERALD

UNBELIEVABLY KIND

Colleen Kidd, Calgary Herald
Extreme Kindness Tour members, from left, Chris Bratseth, Val Litwin, Brad Stokes and Erik Hanson, balance a collection of stuffed animals they are to deliver to the Salvation Army and the Centre of Hope today. The quartet is on a cross-country motorhome tour to do random acts of kindness. See story, Page B3.

During the letter writing we meet a photographer from the *Calgary Herald* who is supposed to do an interview at a nearby café with a woman from Calgary who had been in Manhattan a year before, but he has been stood up. He covers our cause instead.

The photographer doesn't say much, but the speed at which he's clicking pictures suggests he is glad to have stumbled across our scene. He asks a few terse questions without stopping the shoot.

"Looks like you guys are having fun," he grins from behind the camera. "How are Calgarians likin' the love?"

Erik leaps at the chance to answer with a pun: "We're really sticking it to them today and nobody seems to be able to shake the kindness. People we bumper-stickered ages ago are still advertising a gentler world!" The photographer groans, but scribbles down the quote anyway.

Chris is on the ground covered in Post-it Notes and looks appropriately ridiculous for the camera. The note sticking to his forehead says, KIND FOR LIFE: I PROMISE.

Val and Erik have kindness covered with goodwill Post-it Notes for Calgarians.

"It'll be nice to tell a fun story for a change," the photographer admits with a sigh.

We couldn't have said it better ourselves.

Later in the day we're off to the Salvation Army's Centre of Hope. Some network cameras have come along for the ride and the energy in the kitchen as we serve food is upbeat.

The halls are full of people reading, a sign that affirms our impression that the shelter worked hard to create an atmosphere that promoted growth and learning, that is, sustainable healing rather than a quick fix. The Centre of Hope is a beautiful facility, a happy side effect that expedites the inner healing process. Steven, an ex-heroin user,

Erik and Chris serve it up at the Salvation Army's Centre of Hope.

tells us that the Salvation Army is responsible for his recovery.

"This is where I come to feel good about myself." Steven tugs at his blond goatee and continues. "The building is clean and bright and it makes me feel like that on the inside, too. I even dress up when I come here — to try and set an example." Steven brushes his jeans. "Even if I just end up peeling carrots for three hours I like to show my thanks by looking good."

It is the first time I've heard of a building committing a random act of kindness.

RED DEER — CHRIS

We are on the road again, whipping past farmers' fields, the dusk of morning slowly giving way to light that spreads across massive bundles of hay shading the fields. Near-gale-force winds batter the bus, incessantly pushing it into the wrong lane. Brad is reluctant to raise the speedometer over a crawl in these extreme conditions. Our speed — or lack of it — has made us late for an interview with a radio station. We place an en route call to the station's D.J. in Red Deer to explain our tardiness. I imagine the locals, sitting at their breakfast tables, coffees in hand, shaking their heads at the thought of four boys from B.C. who somehow made it through the Rockies but can't negotiate the straight highway from Calgary to Red Deer.

When we finally reach our hotel — the Red Deer

Lodge — we are hurried into a conference room where the smiles of a hundred morning diners greet us. In the back of the room reporters juggle pencils and pads; cameras are stationed at shoulder height. At the front of the room our table is cluttered with name tags, microphones, a power point projector and a 16-foot screen. It appears that breakfast will be more than just juice and pancakes — we'll have to speak with our mouths full! We weren't expecting to have to eat and speak, and with no notes or outline we'll have to wing it. After a quick huddle we bound onto the stage, and Erik orders the group to stand up for some callisthenics to energize the audience.

"Instead of just talking about kindness and compassion, I want you to experience the joy of being kind, right now! Everyone, find a partner and face each other. Raise your hands in front of you at shoulder height. Now lunge slowly toward your partner and put your hands around their neck. That's right, strangle them! Oh wait. Sorry, those were the directions for a random act of violence. Uh, scratch that."

Laughter erupts from the staff as they mock the frustrations of the previous day with their co-workers.

"OK everyone, face the side wall. Hands on the back of your partner's neck this time. Now gently massage using your thumbs! You've just turned that act of violence into an act of kindness."

Mid-massage, Val takes the microphone from Erik and talks to the staff about what we would like to accomplish while in Red Deer.

"Our mission over the next three days is simple: we

want to help! However, there is one catch: we'll need your help. No one knows this town like you do. Can anyone suggest an organization, person, or family that could use some kindness?"

No hands rise and most people look down at their breakfast, trying to avoid eye contact. Brad knows a shy audience when he sees one, so he walks into the audience to prompt some suggestions. "Maybe there are people here who need their houses cleaned."

Scores of hands leap into the air. Brad continues to walk through the crowd, a preacher giving a sermon to a congregation of kindness-starved parishioners.

I watch from the front table and spy a woman cautiously surveying the room. She raises her hand in front of her face, not quite high enough for others to see. Brad turns toward her and nods his head.

"I would love to have my house cleaned, but there is someone who needs help even more! Last week a single woman living in a trailer park had her home destroyed by a fire. Tragically, she has no insurance, and her trailer is beyond repair. The only way that she can expect to recoup any money is to move her trailer off the property. She has no family to help her salvage what is worth saving, and no money to move the trailer. Maybe you could help her?"

"Thank you for the suggestion, we will definitely try!" Brad replies.

We had a full day of service planned with the hotel staff and our itinerary barely left us time to have lunch, but we wanted to find a way to make time for this woman who was obviously in desperate need of help. Our only hope was to push quickly through all of our activities to make time for this woman at the end of our Kindness Marathon.

After breakfast, the barrage begins. We head to a central warehouse to pack non-perishables for shipment to other food banks in the province. The food bank is large enough to supply the many small farm communities and families that surround the town. People from all walks of life — young families with infants, transients passing through town looking for work, once prominent community figures who have fallen on hard times, the mentally ill, those who can barely feed themselves, children with less than one square meal a day, the elderly with no family — will receive food and relief from this service. We are overwhelmed by the immensity of this operation, but grateful to be part of it.

Amid forklifts, we set up makeshift work lines, each of us gloved and armed with box-cutters and felt markers. The sorting, marking, and packing can be tedious and tiring, but we know it is a necessary part of this massive production. Although the task borders on dull, I am surprised when I look up from my station to find that every face on the line wears a smile. Each box I date and repack I imagine as a Christmas present, a gift that will be given to a family in need.

We work with great speed and efficiency, knowing that the sooner we have completed our work, the sooner we can get to the woman mentioned that morning. Our

Chris loads pallets of donated produce at the food bank.

frantic pace infuses the workspace with energy. Brad wraps boxes at the speed of an elf on Santa's assembly line, Erik is now running the forklift (into everything in sight), Val is carefully sorting hundreds of boxes of cereal, and I, well, I end up in the hospital, head back, doctor's tweezers prodding my eye.

"There it is! It looks curved . . . quite grainy . . . and there we have it. Not what I expected, but better than glass. Mr. Bratseth, you have an interesting object lodged in your eyelid. It looks like cereal. Yes, a chunk of Cheerio to be exact!" the doctor explains, chuckling under his mask.

When I catch up with the Crew I am told that they have moved from packing food to grooming felines at the SPCA. Most of the animals are timid once taken out of their cages, and we are forced to wrangle them into tubs to administer a mandatory scrubbing. The smell of wet-mongrel makes its way into our clothes and their hair sticks to our skin. Erik is in charge of containing the unruly dogs and the bathing room is drenched.

The workers do as much as they can to soothe the animals' stress and keep the bugs at bay, but what the dogs really need is a home. We try to focus our energy on the volunteers, who work to provide comfort and security for the animals until they're claimed. We hope that those who volunteer here feel recognized and appreciated for their ongoing commitment.

Chris goes to the dogs — now that's a good hair day!

In our motorhome, we track down the woman who has had the fire and survey the skeleton of her trailer. The only solid structure left on her property is a nine-foot dumpster filled to overflowing with the remains of her possessions, a lifetime of memories and savings taken first by the fire and now by this box. Sue, a single woman in her forties, waves and leads us inside. We duck our heads as we enter, weary of any potential hanging wires slithering down the walls. It feels like a child's tour through a haunted house. Each corner reveals another frightful reminder of the destruction. Melted plastic curls over exposed walls. Insulation, like blackened cotton candy, hangs over support beams, and deformed toys (luckily no children were present to witness the destruction) lie atop a soot-covered bed. Almost everything has been tainted by the smoke and drenched by the water used to quell the fire. Like her soaked pictures lying in soggy shoeboxes, this experience has stained her forever.

Brad covers his mouth with his shirt to guard against the gases and dust that linger and asks, "Where were you when this happened?"

"I remember running down the hall — the flames were licking the ceiling, forcing me out. All I had time to grab was my cat. By the time I was outside, the flames were blocking the door, but I managed to get out. It was a terrifying lesson and one I want to share. Some of my friends have brought their children over to see first-hand how dangerous and devastating a fire can be. I want them to see what can happen."

Sue continues the tour, then gives us our orders.

"Unfortunately, everything has to go. I can't carry the beds and dressers, so could you boys help me move them?"

That's why we are here. I just wish we could do more. I wish we had more resources to help: money, time, or friends that we could refer her to. Unfortunately, we are in a town in which we have few connections. I hope we can help her today and motivate someone else to follow in our footsteps tomorrow.

Like a line of volunteers sandbagging a riverbank, we ferry most of the larger items out of the home. Our hands look like we have finished a day in a coal mine and are stained with the soot that blankets everything in the building. Outside, the pile of charcoaled items grows to its limit. Looking at the black mountain of debris, Brad proposes an absurd but hilarious activity for all of us.

"I think what we need is to have some fun!" he exclaims, then jumps up onto the bin full of Sue's belongings. "Sue, grab my hand, I need you up here for a minute."

Brad holds Sue by the hand and starts to jump up and down on the mattresses. Like children on a trampoline they squash the contents. Each crash underneath draws a giggle. Her perspective changes with every bounce. After catching her breath, she climbs down and leans against the bin.

"I had no idea I would have this kind of help. I am incredibly grateful to all of you. My neighbours have been really supportive, but I really didn't want to burden them with this. The only thing is, I'm at a loss as to what I should do with what I can salvage. I have no place to put it so I am not going to keep anything. I don't need all of these things I have. This is a new beginning."

A van pulls up with a reporter who has come to cover the story for the local news. After filming a piece with the Kindness Crew at the food bank, he had agreed to shoot this story so others in the community will learn about Sue's situation. Fifteen seconds on the nightly news won't be much, but hopefully someone will pick up where we leave off.

The reporter tries to reassure her that everything will be all right. "Someone will certainly respond. People in Red Deer pride themselves on taking care of each other. This story will be in every living room in town tonight. It's a rallying call."

We leave Sue and Red Deer knowing that although we can't stay and help there are others that can and hopefully will. Our journey continues, as does hers.

EDMONTON — BRAD

The morning press conference is our best one yet, thanks to the addition of wireless microphones that make me feel like a Las Vegas lounge singer or stand-up comedian as I prowl through the crowd attacking the back rows with hugs, songs, and massages. No longer confined behind the podium, our press conferences have now taken on a whole new energy.

After the conference we head to The Children's Hospital, a facility surprisingly free of the depressing atmosphere I've noticed in other hospitals. The halls are full of laughter, colour, music, and beauty, and a *Patch Adams* approach to medicine seems to rule the day. The children adore the stuffed animals and autographs from the Edmonton Eskimo offensive linebackers, who walk away more inspired than the children after the encounter. The sight reminds me of the time my mother was undergoing chemotherapy and gained strength from a six-year-old girl sitting beside her receiving the same treatment. A day spent with the young patient was enough though to help my mother learn how to laugh and let go of some of the anger, bitterness, and resentment that had hardened her against hope.

Another place filled with the sound of children's laughter is the West Edmonton Mall, a city-sized collection of indoor stores, restaurants, water parks, skating rinks, and roller coasters. Chris persuades a man in charge of skate rentals to donate a few to those in line and offer free skating for the next 10 minutes.

Meanwhile Val approaches the manager of a nearby diner and asks if we can wash dishes, mop the floor, wipe the counter, clear tables, make milkshakes, and fry burgers. We make a towering milkshake for one of the employees to demonstrate our skill, but are pulled away in aid of a 60-year-old Russian wonder named Piotr who is giving skating lessons to anybody in earshot. It is easy to see how much he enjoys sharing his talent and passion

The Crew on sundae detail at a West Edmonton Mall diner.

with other people. His excitement reminds me of Erik, minus a Russian accent, when he is talking about surfing to someone who is considering trying it for the first time.

During the course of the afternoon we convince a retired opera singer to perform for the crowd, treat some fellow mall customers to a free roller coaster ride, and then head to the next destination, dinner and bed.

The next morning I find myself several miles west of Edmonton at a buffalo ranch. I am hanging on for dear life to the outside rail of a Jeep Explorer as we speed across raw uncut prairie ahead of a herd of galloping buffalo. Erik maintains that we are making the meat leaner. I will have to remember to take my friend Milan, who owns the ranch, to a salmon farm in repayment. Milan, unfortunately, does not have much work left for us to help out with. We are a week late for the yearly fall round-up and the ranch is settling in for its winter slumber. Opting to explore some of the surrounding fields, we are amazed by the size of the buffalo and elk on the ranch. I imagine what it must have been like when these creatures freely roamed the prairies of North America. The world seems so much smaller now, smaller than I imagined as a child growing up with dreams of playing for the Edmonton Oilers. Then Calgary was the edge of the world, now it is just a dot on a much bigger map.

Visiting Milan's ranch is like coming home after 15 years. The smells are the same and the trees and earth feel familiar to my touch. The place reminds me of summers with my sister, of being awakened by my mother in the middle of the night to warm some newborn calves whose mother had died. I remember Mom's kindness to animals, her laughter, her happiness. Our stay in Alberta has been tough on me; it's made me vulnerable to painful thoughts that seem to surface more frequently here, but perhaps it has also enabled me to let go of recent memories and reclaim the happier past of my childhood. I expect it has also helped me to see my future more clearly.

Helping People in Crisis

1. Rally your crew!

With your family, co-workers, or schoolmates issue a challenge to others to help those in crisis in your community. Assemble people who are moved by this task, who make you laugh, who you like to spend time with. Look to these people for assistance. In the face of a major crisis it's amazing how people band together. That bond is created because the task at hand means something to you. Bring your passion to it and people will follow with their own. The chance to arrange a crew of people and work on a positive project could arise at any time, so be willing to run with it. If you are really committed to creating positive change you must be able to tread the fine line between planning ahead and embracing the spontaneous. If you over-plan you will lose some of the magic but if you simply leave it up to chance you may find it hard to get anything done.

2. Get your story in the press!

Write a letter to the editor of your local paper challenging locals to help others in need — cite concrete examples of how they can do this. Finding a project is not hard. You may not even have to look. Get together with your crew and brainstorm how you can help. Do what you can. Remember, your imagination is often your biggest asset. Be open to new and unique ideas that people within the Crew present.

3. Find a champion!

Approach an individual or a group featured in your community media that could help. Volunteer your time, donate money, and spread the word about the cause by working with this organization.

4. Listen to what is needed.

Take the time to *listen* to those who need help. Ask them what would improve their situation the most. Don't take anything for granted. Then do something for them to thank them for their thoughts — take them out for dinner or design a card for them. Let them know that you care.

5. Tell your story!

Tell everyone you know. If you want to create something bigger, involve as many people as possible and get them to pay it forward by telling people about what they're doing. This type of publicity introduces you to resources you never knew you had and solves problems that once seemed beyond you. Email us at thecrew@extremekindness.com. By documenting your adventures in altruism you will inspire others to take up the challenge.

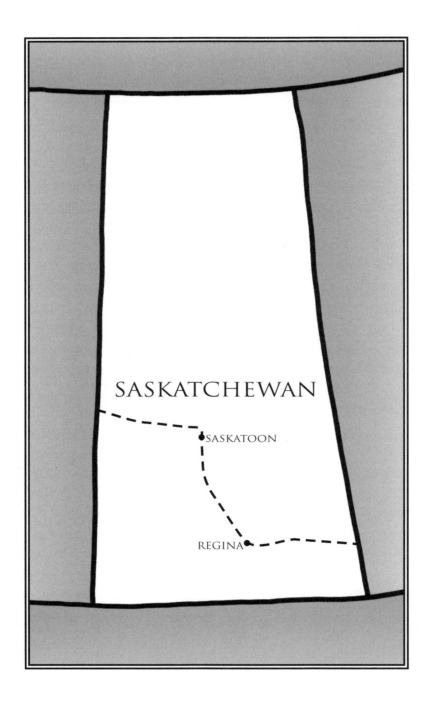

SASKATCHEWAN

No act of kindness, no matter how small,
is ever wasted.

— Aesop

SASKATOON — ERIK

This morning, like many others on the tour, I am uncertain and groggy. At an hour too early to mention, electronic ringing breaks the silence. A bleary-eyed figure desperately plows through books, dirty T-shirts, and kindness supplies in search of the offending phone.

"Hello," he croaks.

"Uh, just a minute . . ." and then, holding his hand over the receiver, "Who wants to take this? Does anyone want to take this? Hey, can someone else take this?"

Val stands on the bed in his Calvin Klein's, phone in hand, appealing to the sleeping masses — it's a pretty funny sight to behold, unless, of course, you're pretending to be asleep.

"Geez guys, I can't go on the radio like this."

Val spends the next 10 minutes on hold, performing Pavarotti vocal exercises.

Following the radio interview, Kelly, our videographer, coughs his way out of the squeaky hideaway bed, slams open the RV door, and attempts to find the nearest public washroom. The motorhome washroom is strictly and wisely off limits for the entirety of the tour, apparently due to "plumbing issues." The rest of us wallow in the stuffy air of the motorhome trying to remember exactly how we had arrived wherever we were. Slowly it comes back to us. We had arrived in town too late to check into the hotel and had given up finding a local host in lieu of parking in the lot across the street from the Radisson. The whole thing was a bit embarrassing.

My expectations for Saskatoon are low. From the looks of the map it is flat, dry, and boring. Seriously, what kind of adventure can we get into in a city like this? Some have described the city as "the Paris of the Prairies," a vibrant metropolis with friendly people, a thriving arts scene, beautiful architecture. I am prepared to revise my opinion, but the city will have to prove itself interesting if it wants an upgrade.

The Radisson Saskatoon, our home for the next few days, backs onto the North Saskatchewan River and is nestled beneath one of the seven striking bridges that connect the city. The broad river is flanked by green space with walking and running trails ranging from paved Victorian walkways to hardened dirt paths. I am eager to go exploring but first things first.

After check-in and unpacking, every housekeeper, receptionist, and concierge crams into the tiny lobby conference room for the staff rally. After briefly explaining the logistics of a Kindness Marathon and how tomorrow will shape up, we launch into a series of videos and photos compiled from the last month of touring. These clips are an attempt to convey the energy and humour associated with marathons. The Merrit clip Kelly has just finished editing causes the room to fill with laughter as Brad and I are pictured attempting to tame wild horses.

The rally also includes theatre games, which provide the opportunity for associates to perform random acts of kindness in a closed, comfortable environment before taking it to the streets the next day. "Who's line is it anyway?" is a game we play, borrowed from the popular television show, in which the audience is encouraged to create a setting, characters, and a problem to be solved through kindness.

We spend the rest of the afternoon and evening editing video clips and gathering supplies for the next day. Balance is key if we hope to maintain a high level of energy so, knowing we have a big day ahead, we hit the sack early.

Early the next morning we emerge from our rooms wearing bright yellow Kindness Crew T-shirts and jogging gear, a product of a pairing with Frontrunners, a Victoria running store. The shirts were created for the very first Kindness Marathon in which Frontrunner employees joined the Kindness Crew and took over Victoria like a pack of bumblebees, pollinating the streets with good-will. The four of us decide to take that same energy to the chilly streets of Saskatoon.

Before our press conference at 9:00 a.m. we jog down-town to stay warm and to accomplish as many acts of kindness as possible. Our first candidate is a young woman studying hairdressing at a local school. Apparently the students are in need of models, so faster than you can say Vidal Sassoon we follow her into a salon with a check-ered tile floor and an overpowering aroma of hairspray. Within a matter of minutes I am styling the students' hair, Brad is assisting with perms, Val is having his hair washed and styled, and Chris is busy cutting a student's hair and demonstrating what *not* to do.

Our next stop is the lobby of the Hotel Senator, an old wooden building staffed by two boisterous women. Both have seen us in the media and are tickled to pass us a few rags and the orange-scented Pledge wood polish. Within minutes we have blitzed the lobby, polished nearly all the wood, and caused a few blushes with heartfelt hugs.

Down the street from the hotel, Saskatoon's finest are standing in front of a local coffee shop. We approach the R.C.M.P. officers, strike up a conversation, and ask if they have a project for us.

"There're a few officers back at the station who I'm sure could use a hug," one jokes. "Actually, if you really want an interesting perspective, there's someone who could use some kindness. He's always got something to say," he says, pointing to a tall, thin, well-bundled man looking like a cross between Icabod Crane and Keith Richards.

The man they introduce as Keith lopes around the side of the building carrying a large garbage bag full of pop cans. Keith is one of Saskatoon's less fortunate and has been living on the streets for years. We know he needs kindness but are reluctant to embarrass him with a direct offer for fear that that would assume too much.

Though kindness is something that transcends religion, culture, language, and class we too often jump to the conclusion that the most needy will most readily accept it. Strangely, kindness is something everyone wants to give and few want to receive. Don't believe it? Try paying someone a genuine compliment today. Nine out of 10 times the person will attempt to deflect or deny it. Through past tour experiences we've learned that often the best way to initiate a conversation with someone who appears to be in need is to reverse the dynamic and ask the person to help *us*. We structure our questions to allow us to accept the random kindness of strangers as well as to offer it.

"Keith, do you know anyone on the street who could use a random act of kindness?"

After a diatribe about the state of the downtown core and its inhabitants, he suggests that the city itself could use some cleaning. We follow him to a neighbouring alley and find rotting garbage spilled across the potholed cement. Trying to hold our breaths, we collect the garbage and heave it into a nearby dumpster. Opportunities for random acts of kindness don't always present themselves in the manner you think they will. Sometimes it means empowering someone else to create the change they want to see in the world.

A block from the hotel, three young men and one older man are unpacking office equipment from a large truck.

"Let me help with that," I say, grabbing one end of a heavy oak desk. Chris, Brad, and Val grab oversized chairs and large office partitions. They can't see anything wrong with our offer, so without skipping a beat, they continue working. When the job is done we thank them, they thank us, and we hit the showers at the Radisson to prepare for our press conference.

The press conference goes off without a hitch and after the proceedings several local media reporters (including one from a radio station doing a live broadcast from the hotel), staff members from other local hotels, members of the community, and the local MP swarm onto 4th Street under a shower of hail and begin to offer passersby hot drinks, fresh-baked muffins, Radisson umbrellas, and multi-coloured carnations. The hotel employees set up an old-style shoe shining station and while Val is giving out flowers, Brad gives hand massages to parking attendants, and Chris stands in the middle of the street stopping passing cars to distribute warm poppy seed and blueberry muffins.

I head up 20th Street with two enthusiastic hotel volunteers offering muffins, hugs, compliments, and coffee to anyone we pass. The two women stop every person on the street and do whatever they can to brighten their day. The dynamic duo directs me toward a local farmers' market where they're sure we can rustle up some action. The market is packed with people, but by this point we are too far from the hotel to restock supplies and are down to our last muffin. Part of the beauty of a Kindness Marathon is its spontaneity; when the supplies run out, the energy and the enthusiasm are still in full force and the possibilities are endless.

I approach one of the vendors selling yellow and white daisies the size of my head and offer her the last muffin.

"All right, what's the catch?" she asks.

"No catch," I say. "It's just a random act of kindness, although if you wanted to pass on some of those beautiful flowers to another vendor in the market I would be happy to deliver them for you." I smile.

She smiles. "Here you go. Take them to that couple over there selling the bread."

After presenting the flowers to the surprised couple I describe the tour, relate some of our recent adventures, and explain how we're trying to make the most of our limited resources at the market. The couple send me across the market, Bundt cake in hand, to offer to the woman at the honey table.

In the space of an hour the kindness has been transformed into a homemade berry pie, a foot-long cucumber, a bag of fresh tomatoes, a half-dozen oatmeal cookies, a bag of white beans, a bunch of fresh herbs, a bag of beer nuts, and a fresh baked loaf of bread. All from one muffin and a great idea. Such is the power of paying it forward.

We return to the hotel just in time to join a group of people bent on storming the police station with coffee and baked goods. Chris is leading the pack and intends the Kindness Crew to distribute cookies, muffins, hot chocolate, massages, and hugs to the "officers back at the station who could use a hug." In my experience, law enforcement officers do not, as a whole, tend to embrace random, unauthorized filming and hugging inside their headquarters. Nevertheless we enter the police station like a band of merrymakers that, if discovered on the street late Friday or Saturday night, probably would have been heading through those very same doors in hand-cuffs and with a police escort.

However, the French-Canadian officer at the front desk seems unperturbed and even slightly amused when we offer the chief of police a massage. Officers who poke their heads into the hallway are ambushed with hugs and warm beverages, then send us off in search of exceptionally surly comrades and overworked desk jockeys who could use some cheering up. The switchboard operators are ideal candidates. "They sit on stiff chairs all day in a dark, stuffy room. They could definitely use some kindness."

Several blank faces look up from enough electronic gadgetry to rival the bridge of the Starship Enterprise. For the next five minutes we pamper the shocked officers and chat with them about our kindness tour. It occurs to us that what we are doing could potentially make their jobs easier — happier people make for fewer crimes. The officers agree, admitting that they are so often *reactive* they don't have time to be *proactive* and work for change. We leave the control room buoyed by the conversation and filter out of the station.

Absorbing a lesson in compassion from Mahatma Gandhi in Saskatoon.

Chris has convinced the local costume shop to loan us outfits for the rest of the day. Chris is Kris Kringle, I am a giant yellow chicken, Brad is an elf, and Val is a horse. When we emerge onto the street, cars honk, people point and laugh, and wherever we go the crowd parts. At the Midtown Plaza Mall on 1st Avenue we begin giving away CDs, insoles, hats, hugs, massages, basically anything we managed to dredge up from the storage compartments in the motorhome. Chris, with 15 kids in tow, is carrying all the freebies through the mall in a giant sack, Brad is commandeering shoppers of any age for a singalong, I am chasing giggling elderly women around the jewellery section of The Bay trying to distribute hugs, and Val is just trying to stay cool in his heavily padded costume.

The scene is surreal to say the least. Needless to say, we only manage to elude mall security for about 20 minutes before we are escorted, albeit kindly, from the premises.

Outside, a roaming CTV van drives past, travels about a block, slams on the brakes, and fires in reverse to investigate. The six o'clock news crew is looking for local colour, so for the next hour they film our spontaneous antics. The cameraman admits this is one of the best assignments he's had since starting with the station. We saunter into a local clothing store and try to help the clerks by folding clothes. Customers cannot refrain from staring and are nabbed by CTV for the "shocked bystander interview."

We head back out onto the streets and down an alley where a local band is doing a photo shoot for their new album. They literally needed some colour, so we pose in several of their shots while the news crew gets some visually striking "on the street" footage.

From the alley we move to Ming's Kitchen, a Chinese restaurant down the street, where we chop lettuce and make spring rolls for the impeding dinner rush. The CTV guys nab a few more action shots in the kitchen before hurrying back to the newsroom to edit the piece.

After a quick snack and friendly conversation at Ming's we head back to the hotel to meet   Jonathon. When we arrive he is sporting a green mohawk wig and has been chatting with Iona, an elderly woman who has asked the Crew to accompany her to visit some friends at a local retirement home.

Once there, we walk the sterile hallways past

crocheted wall hangings to a dining room where we are greeted by half a dozen of the residents. Despite differing levels of awareness, everyone has a story to tell or something to teach us. We sit around a table as dinner is served and watch the local news. Mid-program our story comes up and although the folks are vaguely interested, they seem unimpressed. The real excitement and energy occurs when we speak to them one on one. I thought they would be excited to see us on TV, but then I realize they can flip on the TV and observe the outside world any time they want, what they can't "flip on" is real conversation. We turn off the TV and spend the next hour or so talking instead.

After dinner, Chris, part Santa Claus part Elvis Presley, leads us, guitar in hand, through the maze of hallways like a troupe of roaming minstrels. I fall behind the Crew and meet a silent elderly woman who agrees to a game of shuffleboard. Playing shuffleboard while dressed as a yellow chicken was one of the most surreal moments I have experienced. I highly recommend it.

In the Alzheimer's wing we split up, to interact with someone one on one. Chris is playing a piano duet with a gentleman named Howard. Brad is strumming the guitar for a small but rather boisterous audience. Val and Kelly are conducting interviews with whoever will join them on the couch, and I am listening to Bill describe the farm where he lived with his wife. Suddenly in a panic he asks me where she is. A nurse discreetly informs me that his wife passed away years earlier. It can be a difficult and even painful process to connect with someone suffering from a debilitating illness, but never pass up the opportunity to comfort someone who feels so alone. Their life experiences are invaluable — learn from them, they just may change your perspective.

We reluctantly leave the wing and head back to the hotel in the dying rays of the evening sun. Dawn to dusk. Our obligation as Kindness Crew members is officially over, but our obligation as good friends has just begun. David Crow, our writer, is celebrating his 29th birthday.

David is part Ernest Hemingway, part J-Crew model, and part superhuman. His accounts of the tour for the Web site also involve filming, taking pictures, and doing research. Tonight it is our chance to celebrate all that. After dinner we play the Compliment Game, taking a minute to say what we genuinely appreciate about the other members of our crew, but we focus primarily on Dave. It's a great exercise that reminds each of us to appreciate our friends and to accept genuine compliments.

My puffy eyes (it had been a late night on the town) are stinging. We meet over a lazy midday brunch, confirm our obligations, brainstorm ideas for an American tour, and review the agenda, which includes a stop at the Friendship Inn (a local soup kitchen), and a visit to Walter Marion High School.

Upon arriving at the soup kitchen we draw from years of restaurant experience and quickly join the area that best suits our skill set. Val, Chris, Kelly, and Dave distribute the food to anyone who pulls up a chair and, being the only one with kitchen experience, I am relegated to potato peeling. The lunch rush is frantic to say the least. The logistical nightmare of feeding 150 people in the space of an hour should not be underestimated. We manage to pull off the lunch and most of the clean-up before Jonathon, ever the tour manager, hauls us back to the motorhome and off to our final stop in the city of bridges, Walter Marion High School.

Every time we speak at a new school I feel like I'm 17 again. The kids' energy is electric and those at Walter Marion are no exception. Four guys travelling across the country doing nice things for people doesn't seem like the kind of thing high school students could get excited about, but you'd be surprised. When we speak about why we're doing the tour and the adventures we've had, the kids respond with enthusiasm and begin to share their stories with us. We try to be honest and don't pretend to be something we're not, so that even if they don't like us, they'll at least respect us. We can't expect to connect with everyone, but usually by the end of our presentation most in the audience are motivated to follow our example. Our faith in the kids from Walter Marion is justified — we receive countless emails from them over the course of the tour, each recounting an act of kindness.

REGINA — ERIK

From the top of the only ski hill in Saskatchewan we look back at Saskatoon and on to Regina. We have discovered Blackstrap Provincial park, a man-made ski hill created for the 1971 Canada Winter Games. After driving the dusty gravel road that follows the lake (created by digging the dirt now stacked in a 500-foot hill directly beside it) we stopped the motor-home in the parking lot at the base and sprinted, calves burning, to the highest point on the horizon.

Bathed in late afternoon sunlight and neck high in wheat, I turn the camera on Val. "What is one piece of advice you have for someone watching this?" He sits for a moment contemplating and takes a deep breath of the rich prairie air before responding.

"I would say to anyone who is trying to realize a dream, who's encountering any sort of obstacle, who gets beaten down, to persevere and keep the faith. I had a bad start to my day today. I felt awful and I wasn't sure how I was going to turn it around and then nature did it for me."

We are all feeling pretty good right now. An hour before it was another story. The motorhome had been thick with tension leaving Saskatoon. Being confined in the same tight space, continually forced to make decisions for the group that at least one person will object to, and having too few outlets to renew our energy after the marathons is a recipe for disaster. You couldn't move without bumping into someone, packing, and unpacking — it was enough to strain any friendship.

A warm prairie wind whips the top of the hill. Maybe Blackstrap has quenched our longing for the mountains, maybe we just need to let off steam, but suddenly we are kids again, goofing around in front of the camera and laughing *with* each other instead of *at* each other. Val and I use the abandoned chair lift as a giant jungle gym, climbing into it to swing precariously from rusty cables. Kelly and Brad explore the engine shack while Chris and Jonathon look for old ski relics. Val grabs the camera and films my digital diary.

"It's comforting to know that no matter how down or frustrated or lost in my life I might feel, there's always somewhere I can go for inspiration. I think that stems from the fact that there are places like this out there."

Val responds as I flip the camera on him. "This is a perfect example of the kind of thing you miss if you don't take chances. We could have driven past this ski hill tonight, but because we chose to leave Saskatoon early the opportunity presented itself, we took it, and this is one of the highlights of my trip so far."

As we watch one of the most remarkable sunsets in recent memory, a sense of ease and camaraderie not felt since our climb together in Canmore descends upon us. We are once again brothers who can overcome anything — possibly even another night in the motorhome.

We pull up to the Regina Inn mid-afternoon and are greeted by everyone from the hotel including the Kindness Captain, Laura Armitage, and Steve Vallard, the general manager, who greet us in the lobby. One thing that all the CHIP hotels succeed in doing is hiring great staff. Laura is no exception. The lively redhead is full of life and used to "thinking outside the box." This is a woman who can make things happen.

After a high energy staff rally I set out to explore the city and stretch my legs. A scenic path meanders along Wascana Lake through lush parklands and past the Regina Legislative Building. I sprint up the front steps and inside to explore its kindness potential for tomorrow. An official-looking guard turns out to be extremely helpful, and after explaining the tour to her she issues me a visitor pass so that I might search out the building manager. After finding his office vacant I take the opportunity to fully use my pass and explore the nooks and crannies not usually open to the public. It's not until I am stopped and questioned by an irate guard while perusing a room filled with artwork that I end my self-guided tour and head back to the hotel for dinner.

The morning of the Kindness Marathon, Patrick, the hotel's first-class media liaison, arranges several appearances on Regina's "drive to work" radio programs so we load up with fruit platters, baked goods, and coffee and blitz the CJME/Z99 broadcast building. Our efforts pay off threefold: we perform kindness to strangers; we create an electric buzz in the radio station; and Regina commuters enjoy a day brightened by four boys from the coast.

The intersection in front of the Regina Inn is madness. If you happened to be caught at a red light at the corner of Victoria and Broad on the 26th of September between 10:45 a.m. and 1:00 p.m. you will remember it. The combination of 50 people in Kindness Crew T-shirts, traffic-stopping fresh muffin and tropical fruit deliveries, and enthusiastic hotel associates in the street encouraging large trucks to honk for kindness was a sight not soon forgotten. Our lackadaisical interpretation of the city traffic law summons the presence of a Regina city police patrol car, but instead of berating us, the officer slows down, honks his horn, whoops his siren, and waves. We can do no wrong.

Steve Vallard has rounded up several of the trolleys that might normally be used to transport baggage and packed them with squeegees, shammies, and car shampoo. Several more associates are quickly pulled from their tasks in the hotel and mobilized for a free car wash. Brand new BMWs and rusted pickups alike pull in for the royal treatment. The owners are fed, entertained, and interviewed; some even join the fun and pitch in to clean other cars.

Meanwhile, Kelly and Brad are fast-talking the security guard at a government building across the street into granting us free access so we can hand out roses to office workers on the upper floors, including a window washer, who has been cheering us on from several stories up.

Brad's government office excursion inspires me to suggest we continue our good deeds for the civil servants of the provincial capital by returning to the Legislative Building I had scouted yesterday. The rest of the Crew agrees and after a photo shoot on the front lawn we are once again granted security passes to explore the extensive network of marble hallways, looking for Dave, the building manager. Dave's office is decorated with posters of Clint Eastwood and more Pez dispensers than I have ever seen. Although good-natured, he instantly senses an air of tomfoolery and after informal introductions cautions us against anything loud or too explorative. He goes over a long list of rules, then passes us on to Steve, the most well-informed tour guide/babysitter in the building.

Steve, a middle-aged and soft-spoken maintenance man, takes us up a tight stone spiral staircase to the tower. From the outside it is the most striking feature of the building, but from the inside it is just a domed room filled with dust and old supplies. After much persuasion and the radio OK from Dave we are led through a gate and up an ancient wrought-iron staircase that snakes precariously several hundred feet up the inside wall of the dome. We emerge into a smaller, dustier room with another staircase leading to what looks like a tiny dome. Steve leads the way and unlocks the final rusty door. We emerge onto a small walkway that circumnavigates it.

A view of Regina explodes beneath us and air fills our lungs. We are privy to a breathtaking view normally reserved for maintenance men and the local waterfowl. Four distinctive red lights adorn the top of the building and distinguish it from any other on the Regina skyline. Brad, the first to round the dome, notices that one of them is burnt out. I hustle back down the stairs and grab a replacement bulb from old box I had seen on the way up. I screw in the red bulb and stand back to marvel at our work — now thousands of people will see the fruit of our labour.

Downstairs, we wander the halls and offices distributing hugs and massages and escorting several low-level

Surveying the city atop the Legislative Building in Regina.

government employees between offices, a service for the high-ranking members of parliament only.

We leave the seat of government to make a 2:00 p.m. television show called *Talk of the Town*. We arrive at the Access Communications television station with a box of warm chocolate chip cookies for the staff and quickly make our rounds. We are slated to appear during the last 20 minutes of the program, so decide to watch the first half of the show from the control booth. The technicians' professional hands flip expertly over the knobs and buttons and our ever curious videographer, Kelly, soon begins asking questions about how the equipment works. One of the three technicians offers his chair so I take him up on the offer and begin to control the live video feed. This being my first experience as a station tech, I only get his directions right 80 per cent of the time, which means that occasionally the station is broadcasting a shot of the ceiling or the back of the host's head. Meanwhile, Chris provides an alternative running commentary, voicing over the host's questions with his own and sending the entire control room into hysterics.

After 10 minutes of Chris' improvisation and my on-air flubs we are all in stitches. Brad is doubled over in his chair, his face beet-red, when we are beckoned into the studio. We march on stage still harbouring an air of mischief and introduce ourselves to the host. The host is a local city councillor who interviews people from the community and isn't used to spontaneous outbursts from his guests. Chris takes it upon himself to spice things up, nudging Val's leg mid-answer, poking him in the ribs, or staring intensely at his nose only six inches away. This is live television and there are no retakes, which makes it even harder to keep a straight face. We need to try to maintain at least a thin veneer of professionalism, but when Chris lunges at the host's feet to offer him an on-camera foot massage, things get out of hand. I wrestle his shoes off squirming feet, while the host squeals like a little kid, pausing only long enough to announce, "Well, that's about the best thing that's happened all day!"

The interview concludes when the producer walks on set and presents us with Access Television fleece vests as a token of appreciation. On our way out, the technician mutters, "I can't believe it. That's one of the funniest things I have ever seen on camera."

Vic's Steak House, attached to the Regina Inn, makes

one of the best steaks I have ever eaten, and that evening we all enjoy the satisfaction of a good meal after a hard day's work. After a crème brûlée dessert we each head out on our own evening adventures. I go into the lobby bathroom to wash up before exploring the city. Standing in front of the bathroom mirror is a young man wearing a dirty baby-blue tracksuit and as I walk past him he smiles at me. He is washing his face, rubbing his eyes, and slicking back greasy spiked hair. As I wash my hands in the sink he catches my eye in the mirror.

"Hey," he says, again checking out his face in the mirror.

"Hey," I reply.

"My name is Jake." He turns quickly, holding out his hand.

"My name is Erik."

"What do you do, man?"

I tell him about the tour and some of the adventures we have had lately. "Well, Jake, I've gotta take off. Nice to meet you."

"Hey wait, I've got something I want you to have." He pulls out a wad of money wrapped in a silver money clip with two buffalo coins welded to it. He shoves the money in his pants and thrusts the money clip at me.

"I'm Métis and it's part of our tradition that when you meet someone, you're supposed to exchange gifts."

I hesitate and he waves the money clip at me again with one hand and wipes his nose with the other.

"Take it. It's not much, but my dad won it in a poker game and gave it to me. Usually you're supposed to give something to me too, but don't worry about it."

I didn't know what to do. This was a set up of some kind, but I couldn't figure it out. He stood there holding out the clip. I took it. "Thank you."

"Cool." He says.

I spend the next few minutes trying to figure out the scam. What was the angle? How was he going to get me? Was he going to tell the police I had stolen his money? I felt like a country bumpkin who had been ripped off by a city slicker and was too dumb to figure out how.

I leave the money clip on the tire of the motorhome and wander onto Regina's empty streets in search of live music. By the time I return to the hotel Jake is gone and I never see him again. It isn't until I pick up the clip the next morning that I understand: there is no catch. I was the recipient of a random act of kindness but hadn't been ready to accept it. I was suddenly in the same position as every person we had surprised on the tour. *I* was supposed to be the expert in the field and *I* was having trouble believing that a stranger would do something nice for me. I hadn't been willing to give him an opportunity to do something kind because of the way I perceived him. Jake had taught me a lesson.

For weeks a woman named Jill Henry, the cousin of a friend in Victoria, had been emailing and calling us in an attempt to have us speak at her son's school in White City, a rural town two hours outside Regina. Throughout the tour we received speaking requests that we were unable to fill but reasoned that if she put the same kind of energy into her children and their school that she put into contacting us then White City Elementary was worth visiting.

Due to our keen sense of direction it is lunchtime when we arrive, about 20 minutes late. Jill greets us at the door with a smile, and we are quickly hustled into the staff room where we stuff down a hearty lunch and are informed that we are immediately expected to play a soccer match against some very energetic kids. One match turns into three, as the ace athletes push us hard without neglecting to pass the ball or help up someone who has fallen. They thoroughly and good-heartedly whup us, then come over and shake our hands.

We leave the field, quickly change clothes, and head for the gym and an assembly crammed with over 500 high-energy kids, teachers, parents, members of the community, and the mayor. Les Kichula, the school's principal, explains the nature of the crowd in an interview with Kelly later that afternoon. "The support that we've received in our community school is as good as you could possibly get, in the sense that people are willing to give their time and to share and provide whatever support we might need."

The Kindness Crew is the headliner, but by no means the only act. Students parade to the stage to read poetry, receive awards, tell stories of kindness in their lives, and all join in to offer a moving rendition of "Make the World a Better Place." Other community members make speeches and talk about activities in the community and beyond where the school has made a difference. One example is the school's participation in a province-wide SaskEnergy program called Share the Warmth, which involves the collection of warm clothes for people who cannot afford them. The students gather dozens of bags onto the stage to present to the SaskEnergy representatives in attendance.

Throughout the day kids jump in front of the camera. One boy in Grade 5 says, "I read that if you want to have fun for an hour watch TV, if you want to have fun for a day go to an amusement park, if you want to have fun for life, help others."

We wander the hallways, stopping to participate in drama classes, help with Canadian geography, and field questions about the tour. The bell rings and Jill invites us back to her house for a much needed hot tub and some R&R with the adults. By the time we arrive in the Henry driveway, however, the motorhome is swarmed with kids toting hockey sticks and nets. While Kelly and Dave jump at the opportunity to play, Brad leads a dozen of the wildest kids on a guided tour of the motorhome where I happen to be taking a quick nap. I can hear the door squeak open and Brad's best crocodile hunter voice.

"All right kids! Crikey! 'Ere it is. The mighty and exotic Extreme Kindness motorhome. Watch your step, those little beauties are Chris' dirty socks! They look harmless enough but touch 'em once and you're a goner. Up 'ere is the navigator's seat where we plan our routes though the treacherous suburbs of Regina. Watch out! Crikey don't open that door! It *looks* like a normal fridge but we've been growing some rare and toxic species of fungus and mould in there. Now, moving to the back of the motorhome we have. . . . Hello what's this? This is very rare! Kids, if you watch carefully, buried in the back there is the ferocious Erikbeast. Crikey isn't he a beaut! What a specimen! It looks like he's sleeping now, but wake him up and we could all be done for mates!"

Instantly I am rushed by a flurry of arms and kicking feet. I roar awake and fulfill my role as the ferocious Erikbeast amidst squeals of laughter. I wrestle the laughing kids out of the vehicle and am instantly commandeered to bounce on the trampoline. I am also dared to take a dip in the icy pool. The temperature is a balmy 56 degrees Fahrenheit. I plunge in much to the disbelief and delight of the neighbourhood kids and then make a beeline for the hot tub next door.

At 6:00 p.m. we head out with kids and parents in tow for dinner at the Emerald Park Golf and Country Club. We have a big family night out and share our tour adventures. It is a wonderful evening that reminds us that it does indeed take a community to raise a child and that the next generation in White City is well equipped to carry kindness to the next level.

With three days until we are due in Winnipeg, we pack the last of our gear and prepare to head east toward

Brandon after one final stop. We have four free tickets to a Saskatchewan Roughriders game, a parting gift courtesy of Laura Armitage and the Regina Inn.

People pour into the stadium and the crowd is electric, the cool autumn air rife with the smell of hot dogs and beer. We are dressed in our red Columbia jackets so the woman at the ticket counter looks up and asks, "Who are you guys?"

"We're the Kindness Crew and we'd like three more tickets for the game, please."

"Oh yes, I think we have some comp tickets for you from the radio station. Just a minute."

Unbeknownst to us one of the radio stations had put away seven *more* free tickets, eleven in total. On the walk to the gate I manage to give away two of the tickets to a couple of completely baffled fans before a security guard snatches the other two, thinking that I am trying to scalp them.

"I was just giving them away," I plead.

"Yeah, sure you were. Now if you don't want to lose your ticket too, you had better get moving."

Not in the mood to start trouble I bow to authority and join the others. This is the first CFL game we have ever attended and we come prepared to take advantage of it. We have brought our Kindness Protest signs reading: HUG THE PERSON NEXT TO YOU and YOU DON'T HAVE TO BE CRUEL TO BE KIND. Throughout the game we get progressively rowdier. We have hundreds of fans hugging each other and are working with the Roughriders mascot, a giant squirrel, to get the stadium cheering

Chris and a fan urge 10,000 football fans to hug rather than hut.

louder. While Val, Brad, and I wave signs, Chris deputizes a couple of painted fans decked in full football gear, by involving them in a successful campaign to get the entire cheerleading team to hug each other in front of the full capacity stadium. The crowd goes wild. I don't even remember who won, and it doesn't matter. That night, I doze off to the sound of 10,000 people cheering.

Pay It Forward

Brainstorm

Over lunch at work, or tonight at dinner, talk about your idea for a pay it forward project. Challenge others to join in or start their own. Here are some suggestions for kind acts that can be paid forward:

• **Positive Post-it Notes (YOU LOOK GREAT TODAY!)** — Give one to a stranger, co-worker, or friend, complimenting him or her and urging that person to do the same for someone else.

• **Bon voyage cards** — Give departing strangers at the airport a card that wishes them a safe and happy trip and spread your kindness around the globe.

• **Art on the move** — Set up an easel downtown on a busy street corner. Sketch a face, paint a landscape, or write inspiring quotes. Give them to a stranger and have her pay it forward.

• **Door to door** — Perform a kind act for your neighbour and ask him to pass it on. Bake a cake, mow his lawn, or wash his dog! Challenge him to pay it forward in the next 24 hours to a fellow neighbour.

- **Free coffee** — The next time you are buying coffee, buy one for the person behind you in line. Tell the cashier to ask the next person to pay it forward.

- **Secret Santa** — Buy a gift (new or used) and put it in a gift bag. Give the gift to a stranger or friend and ask him to place a new present in the gift bag and pay it forward.

- **Phone tag** — Phone someone you haven't talked to in a while and tell her how much you appreciate her friendship. Ask her to pay it forward by calling someone she hasn't been in contact with in a while.

Send us an email at:
thecrew@extremekindness.com
and tell us how it worked out!

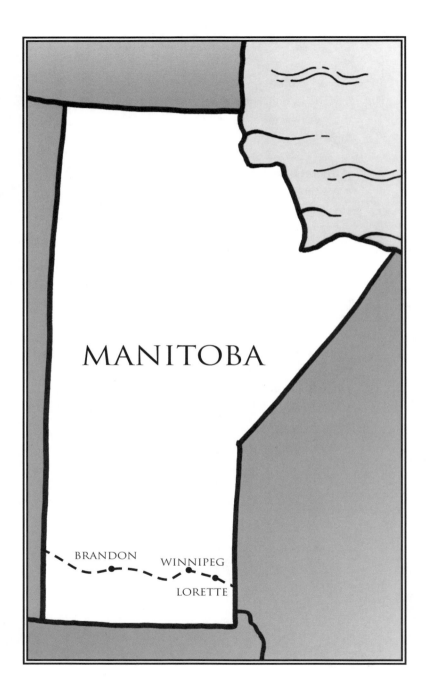

MANITOBA

BRANDON

WINNIPEG

LORETTE

MANITOBA

Guard well within yourself that treasure, kindness.
Know how to give without hesitation,
how to lose without regret, how to
acquire without meanness.
— George Sand

BRANDON — BRAD I am the farthest east that I have ever been in my own country, driving along the straightest stretch of the Trans-Canada after crossing into the friendly province of Manitoba. Dry, grassy, windswept plains are a sleepy mix of green, yellow, and burning red as the sun sets behind us. Within the interior of our rolling bus, a noisy, but good-humoured, debate drags on. We have no obligations until we arrive in Winnipeg in two days. Where should we stop next and spend the night? Erik suggests turning off the beaten track to look for untold stories and good deeds, travelling the side roads of the rural west.

Val wants to take the opportunity to combine media

attention with acts of kindness so that we have something substantial to show our sponsors when we arrive in Toronto. We still need sas Canada to commit to sponsoring the other half of the trip. No media means no sponsors, no trip, no random acts of kindness for the rest of the country.

In Brandon I pull off the highway and refuse to go any farther. The autumn chill has already taken soft command of the early night. We hit up the local grocery store for snacks and information and Val gets advice from a man named William who maps out routes to campsites, restaurants, and a bowling alley. The team splits — Val, Erik, and I for food, the rest to bowl.

At dinner, an older couple sitting in the booth next to us whisper and glance at us, puzzled expressions on their faces. Before I can say anything, the older gentleman rises from his table and walks toward us. He stands beside Erik, who greets him with a huge smile and a nod.

"I don't mean to interrupt, but we couldn't help but overhear your conversation."

I grin sheepishly in apology and open my mouth to assure the man that we will endeavour to be quieter for the duration of their meal.

"Are you young men the same fellows travelling across the country performing good deeds?"

We happily answer that we are indeed, minus one to bowling, the four members of the Kindness Crew. We insist that both Vern and Norma join us for dinner and by the end of our meal we have a place to stay for the night. They also, much to our relief, have the perfect kindness project for the next day. Vern's daughter is in need of some strong backs to fell some trees and remove them from her yard. After weeks of typing and talking and sitting, any physical activity is much appreciated, even, perish the thought, hard honest work. Vern and Norma give us detailed directions to their place and we promise them that we will follow as soon as the bowling professionals return.

People tell us all the time that it is impossible for us to meet and help every person in need around the world. I agree, but we never seem to have any difficulty finding people to help us. For every person I smile at, I receive five smiles in return. We have been in Brandon for less than an hour and already we have been given cheerful directions, a place to rest, and a random act of kindness has been prepared for tomorrow. Who's helping who?

The next day, Norma prepares pancakes, bacon, eggs, toast, and coffee and Vern contacts his daughter and organizes a collection of chainsaws and axes. When we arrive we are joined by the entire neighbourhood. Everyone has come to watch us as Vern, our accomplished foreman, directs his eager, but sadly inexperienced, crew.

Hours later, Val finishes off the last towering oak, and we set to dividing it into small portable pieces. The trees have to be removed for safety reasons, one having hit the house in a winter storm, but Vern will waste nothing. He plans to use the wood for several projects over the next few years. As we come to the end of our job, William, the

"We just want to connect the world through kindness ..."

BRUCE BUMSTEAD/BRANDON SUN

Viewers can find the Extreme Kindness Crew, Val Litwin, Brad Stokes-Bennett, Erik Hanson and Chris Bratseth (left to right) on the Internet at www.extremekindness.com. The foursome updates their web site with footage from the different places they stop.

Kindness crew bowls over locals

By Shelley Vivian
Brandon Sun

If you ever wanted to do something nice for someone out of the blue but never got around to it, here's some inspiration.

The Extreme Kindness Crew, a group of twentysomething do-gooders from Victoria, hit Brandon this weekend as part of its three-month cross-country tour.

The four friends — Val Litwin, Chris Bratseth, Erik Hanson and Brad Stokes-Bennett — have been committing random acts of kindness for the last couple of years but last month, they set out on a tour to spread their benevolence to a wider audience.

"Our message is simple," said Bratseth. "We just want to connect the world through kindness and show people how easy it is to make a change in their own communities."

It didn't take them long to settle in and meet some Brandon folks to whom they could lend a hand.

The gang arrived in the city Friday night and while getting something to eat at a downtown restaurant, they met Verne Kachkowski and his wife, Norma Lennon.

Hearing that the guys needed a place to park their enormous tour motorhome for the night, Verne jumped in and offered them his driveway.

After enjoying breakfast yesterday morning at the couple's home, the kings of kindness asked what they could do for the family in return.

Verne's response? Well, there were a pair of trees at his daughter's house that needed to be chopped down.

So, off they went to Dena Hudey's Seventh Street home, much to her surprise.

"Dad came over and said 'I'm getting

BRUCE BUMSTEAD/BRANDON SUN

Kindness crew member Chris Bratseth films Val Litwin as he cuts firewood with Brad Stokes-Bennett, foreground, during a stop on their Extreme Acts of Kindness Tour in Brandon yesterday.

these trees out' and I said 'OK, I'll help,'" said Hudey.

"He said 'no, I've got these seven guys with me.'"

The four friends travel with a support staff of three.

Hudey was blown away by the random act of kindness.

"It's awesome. It's just like the movie Pay It Forward. And I wanted everyone to know about it because it seems nobody ever hears about the nice things. And there really are nice people left in the world."

Kachkowski agrees. "If it actually caught on across the country, it'd be wonderful."

The kindness guys have knocked on doors offering to cook supper, scrub floors, do dishes, give massages.

They've cut hay on the Prairies and broken horses in B.C.

In Salmon Arm, B.C. they helped establish a record for most spontaneous acts of kindness during an extreme kindness marathon.

A total of 18,321 people in that community committed random acts of kindness in one day.

While the kindness crew has a few sponsors, most of the expense of the tour is coming out of members' pockets.

SEE 'CREW' — PAGE A2

man who had given us advice in the grocery store, arrives. He is a photographer for the *Brandon Sun* and needs a good shot for the front page. We are happy to oblige.

The next morning, on the road again with a newspaper and coffee in hand, I meet a middle-aged woman at a gas station whose tired eyes seem worn with lack of sleep and worry.

"I read about you boys this morning and have been following your journey from day one.

"I smile every time I see you on the news; happy stories are so rare these days. Thank you so much for what you are trying to do. If you have time for one more thing before you go, my sister is dying and she hasn't got very much time left. She'd love a visit; it would mean so much to her. She needs it and so do I."

Memories of my own mother's death are still fresh. I look into the woman's eyes, no longer a mystery, and as teary as my own, and manage to say, "I'm sorry." She turns away from me, knowing what I mean without further explanation. We don't have time to help, but no excuse will make her feel any less alone. I know, because I have felt that same loneliness. Still, excuses to do with schedules and other restraints seem small in the face of death.

I realize that I would remember not only the people I have helped, but also those I could not. On this tour there would be five schools missed for every one that we could squeeze in. For every person I hugged there would be a thousand hugs missed. I hope that friends would take my place and help the woman I watched walk into the cold wind that day. I have to trust that she would find as many people willing to help her as we have found willing to help us.

I look again and realize the woman is no longer in view. I hadn't even asked her name or given her a hug. For that error I can give myself no comfort. Sadly, I had focused on my limitations rather than the opportunity before me.

WINNIPEG — BRAD

I navigate downtown Winnipeg buildings, traffic, above-ground passageways, straight narrow streets, and stop to remember that this is Winnie the Pooh's town. We are en route to the Radisson and I think, as I have many times throughout the course of our journey, how we would have faired without these pit stops.

We are welcomed by signs, banners, and cheerful employees ready for the staff rally. The next day we have an appearance on Breakfast TV; a press conference; volunteer time at a Catholic soup kitchen and a non-profit food bank called The Farmers' Market; a 2:30 p.m. speaking engagement at an elementary school; a 5:30 p.m. interview with the French CBC; and evening chats with reporters from print and radio.

At the largest Catholic Church in Winnipeg, Chris and Erik assemble bag lunches for the hungry while Val talks to Father George about our tour. Father George is Jamaican by birth and his speech is a mixture of the classic English gentleman and Bob Marley. He leads Val and I on a tour of the basement where donated clothes are kept. Val interviews him about his own views on kindness.

"If people wanted to help others, Father, what advice would you give them?"

"We just need people to give, like you boys are doing. We used to have five times as many clothes down here because there was no way to get them to the people. Then a local business donated a van, so they gave us the means to get the clothes on people's backs."

I find it heartening that despite there being many different beliefs, kindness and compassion seem to be core values in most religions. I concentrate on this similarity rather than dwell on the differences. As the Dalai Lama says, "Kindness is simple; kindness is my religion."

At the school later that afternoon we are reminded that young people seem to understand the power of kindness more easily than their elders. The attraction is not its simplicity, cost-effectiveness, or satisfaction; kindness is *fun*. The four of us talk about the different paths we've taken in relation to the kindness movement. Chris begins with who we are, what acts of kindness the tour has committed, and why we are doing it. He plays several media video clips that run off our laptops and also leads them in short interactive games. I talk about how important it is to be kind to others and share the story of my mother's life and death as inspiration. Erik talks to the kids about surfing in the World Championships and how to mix kindness and extreme adventure. Val finishes by explaining the pay it forward philosophy: do something kind of three people and they promise to do the same. Kindness multiplies with each selfless act.

Chris, Brad, and Erik talking to Henry on Winnipeg's CJOB call-in.

During a radio interview that afternoon I am asked about what motivated me to join the tour.

"I suppose my mother's life, and her death, reminded me how beautiful and special life is. Being alive and healthy can be all the power you need to accomplish great things."

Remembering my mother in this way is probably the greatest gift the tour has bestowed. She is my inspiration, rather than a source of sadness. My memories of her are not limited to a woman beaten by cancer and pain, but instead are infused with her smile, her advice, and her pride.

People call the station with comments, suggestions,

and requests; most of them are very positive about what we are doing.

"Can you come and clean my room for me?"

"I would love it if you guys could help me fix my car next week."

"Erik, I need a date to my high school graduation party."

"It sounds too good to be true, come on boys, what's the catch?"

"Could you come to my hockey game this Saturday and cheer for me?"

"What you guys are doing is great, how can I help?"

Chris encourages people to phone the station the following week to respond to the city's cries for help. The last call of the day, however, is different. A soft accent, maybe French, comes over the speakers.

"Allo, my name is Henry and I have been doing random acts of kindness my whole life. I am getting up there in age and am having back, knee, and shoulder problems. My roof is leaking and I need to have it roofed before winter. I live an hour's drive east of Winnipeg in the town of Lorrette. I could really use some help."

Before the radio announcer can reply, Chris leaps in with, "Henry, we will be there tomorrow!"

Henry is overjoyed and promises that food and drink will be waiting. There will always be people who need help and acts of kindness. There will also always be people who need to help others and to give kindness. I have been both types of people in the past and will be both again in the days to come.

Erik hits the roof in Lorette.

LORETTE — BRAD

My shirt is stained with sweat and dirt, my shoulders ache, and my throbbing knees are becoming increasingly bruised from hours of crouching labour. No media, press, or radio reporters have given us an excuse to stop and speak about what we are doing. Oddly enough though, this kind of work is far less tiring than hugging people on the street. Henry has urged us to slow down and rest, but his mid-sized, two-storey home can be re-roofed in a day rather than a week if we push hard enough. Chris and Erik also have a fair amount of roofing experience and they move quickly across the top, working as a team. Val, me, Dave, and

Jonathon are not quite as efficient, but improve by the minute in both quality and quickness. Henry and his two friends have obviously done this sort of work before and give us some handy pointers.

Henry talks, on camera, about what the world would look like if we helped just one person each day. He leans on the chimney and looks off across the vast prairie; a philosopher in a beautiful yet harsh land. He encourages people to work together to make this a reality.

"If we can stop talking at one another and learn to work with one another we can solve any problem. But people forget that and their lives become full of problems and disagreements. This is why kindness is so important. When someone does something nice for you it is a wake-up call for the soul."

That morning we had experienced our own set of problems and disagreements. Chris and Erik are strong-willed so it is no surprise to anyone that they sometimes butt heads; neither man is likely to back down from a confrontation. That day Chris had decided to wear, on camera, a cross-shaped pin given to him by a young student the previous day. Erik felt that Chris was aligning the rest of the Crew with Christianity, which might alienate us from people of other beliefs. The kindness tour is not associated with any religion per se so it is better to be seen as messengers of kindness that everyone can welcome into their hearts and homes. Erik felt Chris was disrespecting the group and its values. Chris thought Erik was overreacting and I admit I felt somewhat the same. Chris was soon claiming that Erik was asking him to deny his own beliefs and told him he was infringing on his religious freedom. This would have been a stronger case if Chris was, in fact, Christian.

I saw merit in both arguments, but by then each party had raised the bar and neither could back down. The stakes were too high. Finally Val, always the problem solver, suggested that tonight might be a more appropriate time to discuss the subject. Chris could wear his pin and if necessary we could edit it out later. Val tends toward negotiation and mediation.

Many of the arguments that arose on the trip were due to stress and cabin fever. Sometimes it seemed easier to find goodness or strength in strangers than in those we knew well. We reduced our friends to their faults and weaknesses, rather than celebrating their accomplishments and strengths.

It took us another hour to finish the roof and then Henry and Brenda summoned us to dinner and a rousing game on *Hockey Night in Canada*. When we take our leave of Henry and Lorette and head west toward Winnipeg for the night, I am edgy because I feel we are going the wrong way. I am in a race to the east, travelling as fast as I can.

As I come to a stop before turning onto the highway I glance back at the interior of our motorhome. Val is typing and Dave is reading while Jonathon watches a movie. Chris and Erik are both asleep on the couch; Chris still has his pin on and Erik wears a dozy smile. All it takes sometimes is a little food, rest, and hockey.

Reaching Out to the Community

1. Come up with an act of kindness.

Each group member has skills that can be harnessed to help others. Ask him what he would like to do and who he would like to help. One Kindness Crew member might be a mechanic and will offer to fix someone's car. Another crew member could have skills as a chef and will propose cooking dinner for an entire family.

2. Contact the media.

Requests for help can be sent to a local media outlet or through www.extremekindness.com. Members of your crew can respond according to their skills, interest, and availability, or your entire Kindness Crew can work together.

3. Tell others what happened!

How was your work received? How did helping others make you feel? How did your school or corporation like the idea? How did the people you helped react? How did your local radio, newspaper, and television station respond to your request? Include all the details.

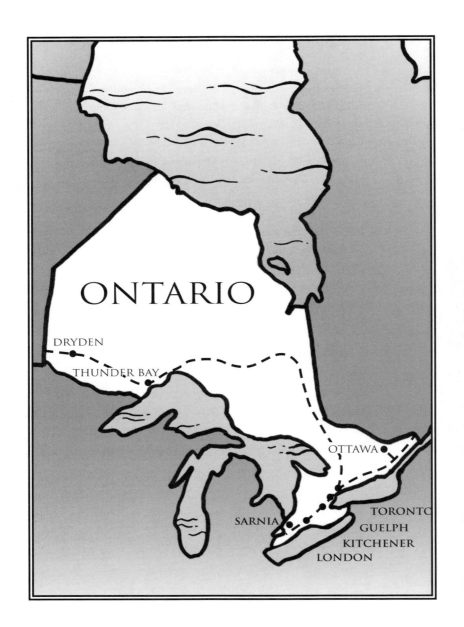

ONTARIO

The ideals which have lighted my way,
and time after time have given me new courage
to face life cheerfully, have been Kindness, Beauty,
and Truth. The trite subjects of human efforts,
possessions, outward success, luxury
have always seemed to me contemptible.
— *Albert Einstein*

DRYDEN — BRAD

We follow Elizabeth in her beaten up, rust-coloured car through the wet and dark streets of a sleeping Dryden. Elizabeth is a local who noticed us attempting to put together a recently purchased portable barbecue, outside the front doors of Wal-Mart. She took pity on us and finished the job in three minutes flat as we held her grocery bags. To thank her we decided it was absolutely necessary to cook Elizabeth and her family buffalo burgers for dinner. She agreed without hesitation, much to my surprise. How do you explain to your family that you have brought home a busload of young men to cook you dinner?

As we enter suburbia, Dryden takes on the feeling of a ghost town. We come to the last street before fields and forest reclaim the land where houses are either half built or ready to be torn down, their driveways just gravel lanes filled with water and potholes. There are no streetlamps on the road, but Elizabeth's small house, also "in progress," looks welcoming in the dim beam of our headlights. Only the kitchen and living room seem to be finished, the rest of the place is a makeshift assembly of unpainted wood, tarps, and boards.

Elizabeth introduces us to her two excited children who wait beside their puzzled father. The picture tugs at my heart. George, Sara, and Steven receive hugs all around and then Sara informs us she is celebrating her sixth birthday that very night.

Erik squats down to her eye level and says in an excited voice, "Did you know that we travelled all the way across Canada to make your birthday? No? Well, that's why we're here, to see you and to cook you our famous buffalo burgers!"

In a few moments Erik has each child holding his hands and showing him their cartoon collections.

Chris tugs at my arm and pulls me aside. "Brad, go and get the stuffed animals we have left over from the last stop."

The stuffed animals in question were donated by the hotel in Winnipeg. I gather up as many as I can find, anxious to help cook the burgers with Val. I enter the house with a loud, "Surprise! Happy birthday, Sara!"

Sara and Steven are beside themselves at the sight of so many toys, two dozen or more. They disappear in a tower of stuffed bears and dinosaurs. We now have the

Val hugs the birthday girl at an impromptu party in Dryden.

extra space we need in the motorhome, Sara has more gifts, and dinner is almost on the table. I agree with Erik more than ever after tonight — the best acts of kindness are almost always random.

THUNDER BAY — CHRIS

Our bus meanders between Dryden and Thunder Bay, pushing toward the invisible midline that divides the country in half. With so much of Canada to traverse, we always seem to be in between press conferences, Kindness

Marathons, and communities. Tired of being stuck in the middle of nowhere, we push steadily into northern Ontario. The only thing that slows our progress in the aching belly of the beast: the motorhome. A mandatory stop is required for refuelling and we take a moment to stretch limbs that haven't moved for seven hours.

Outside, while admiring the natural beauty that surrounds the store, a woman approaches us, promoting the area as if she works for Parks Canada.

"Y'all have come here at the right time — some go to Mexico when it gets cold, but to me these forests are the best that nature has to offer. We come across the border almost every fall," she explains, turning to point at the coloured hills that crowd the highway.

The Ontario fall is extraordinary; the landscape like an impressionist painting swirls and drips colours down our window. Bright bursts of orange, red, and hues of brown freckle the landscape, and reflections from the lakes double the beauty. Driving through this territory has taught us to let the land go and to enjoy it as it passes us by. This makes travelling in the bus a meditative experience, an exercise in appreciating the now. Rather than watching Canada on fast-forward, I wish I could press the pause button and see our country one frame at a time, but our schedule has us again hurtling along the highway to meet deadlines negotiated long in advance.

Inside the bus other territory is traversed. Each person's space has distinct borders; when they are crossed the colonies are sites of unrest. Most of the time though, fingers gently lick magazine pages, headphones deliver concerts for one, eyelids bounce up and down slowing with each jump — sleep is just around the next bend in the road.

Val crams his legs into the small space under the table, cell phone pressing against his cheek, fingers searching systematically through his agenda for the next digits to dial. Dave is in the front seat, legs propped up on the dash. Jonathon's six-foot-five frame takes up every inch of the couch and then some. Kelly, guitar in hand, sprawls across the back bed and strums the songs of the Tragically Hip. Brad is sleeping, curled like a cat in a living room chair, and I thumb through the pages of a novel.

The tides of the great Lake Superior pull the bus forward in two-hour shifts. Everyone must take their turn — no one drives longer, no one drives less. Erik is at the helm and he pushes us full steam ahead.

"Lake Superior is one of the only lakes in the world that can be surfed! I can't wait to see what the swell will be like!" Erik beams.

The only thing that matches Erik's passion for the kindness movement is his passion for surfing. Prior to embarking on the tour, he tried to convince the group there would be enough room in the motorhome for two surfboards (along with gear for three months). When asked where he intended to store the boards, Erik replied matter-of-factly that there was plenty of room to hang them from the ceiling (the six-foot-five ceiling). It took some diplomacy on our part and flexibility on Erik's part to agree that renting surfboards at Lake Superior was a better option.

With only a few minutes of driving between Erik and the great lake, we crest the last hill with Thunder Bay in sight. The view is like looking out over the Pacific. I feel dwarfed by its immensity and blue beauty.

Thunder Bay's mills, malls, and silos wait for us at the foot of the hill nestled among the coniferous forests. The city is an amalgamation of the former Fort Williams and Port Arthur, and is torn at the seams: urban and suburban industry; downtown shops and super malls. We are told it is a city ripe with contradictions, having one of the highest crime rates and also having one of the highest rates of volunteerism in Canada.

The opportunity to visit Thunder Bay presented itself long in advance of our departure. Before leaving, our computer was inundated with letters asking for help from people across the country. Among the emails were a few anomalies — one of them a letter from someone who wished only to be called Mike in Thunder Bay. The email described his commitment to his community, and hinted at a schedule in which his volunteer hours rivalled those spent at work. Mike was definitely a person who put compassion into action and was committed to our mission of connecting the world through kindness. He promised to rally his community if we came. Two weeks prior to our arrival in Thunder Bay we received an itinerary from Mike for our stop in Thunder Bay: 48 hours of non-stop random acts of kindness had been organized. What should have taken a committee to plan and implement, Mike had started on his own, knowing that others from the community would take part once the project was in motion.

A jubilant Mike greets us at a motel on the crest of the city and his enthusiasm for the coming days is palpable. Shock flashes across Mike's face when we step off the bus and surround him for a group hug — our signature handshake! His shock is short-lived; he has waited months for this weekend and the days are planned to the minute. Our schedule would rival that of visiting royalty. The first order of the weekend: a meet-and-greet with the passengers at the Thunder Bay airport.

The airport is the perfect launching pad for our mission to connect the world through kindness. The opportunities to spread our message seem endless, as there are hundreds of potential recipients, both young and old. With only one flight our act of kindness could be carried around the globe. The ripple effect of our kind acts, approaching the speed of sound, could spread across the globe one act at a time. The magnitude of this reach fills each of us with added excitement.

Mike wants to start with visitors — guests first! We position ourselves at the bottom of an escalator that ushers in passengers like a conveyor belt on a production line. Each visitor receives a welcome worthy of a rock star flown in for a one-night performance. Signs sparkle WE LOVE YOU! Roses are passed out and arms are thrown around unsuspecting strangers. Whether a high-five is slapped or a balloon is tied to a baby's arm, when each person walks away their day is a bit brighter.

Then we turn our attention to those who will be leaving. The departure area is crowded with travellers anxious to board their flights. The lines are restless so we break the tension by striking up conversations. Brad chooses to address the audience by standing atop a chair to wish everyone a safe and happy journey. There are a few rolled eyes, but most crack a quick smile.

Val wades into a lineup and chats to a teenager, telling her about paying it forward. "I want you to take this hat as a gift, but this gift is also an investment. I want you to pay this gift forward to three other people once you arrive at your destination. Think of something kind you can do for three strangers and ask them to pay it forward too. Think of the exponential growth! The potential really is unlimited! You have the opportunity here to invest in a kinder world, one act at a time. Think about the impact you could have!"

The 16 year old seems slightly perplexed but excited. "That is so cool. I've never thought of it that way. I will definitely pay it forward! I can start on the plane!" She spoke quickly then turned to run and catch up with her parents.

On a bench near the back of the lineup, Erik sits thigh-to-thigh with a woman dressed in a perfectly pressed designer suit. The palm of her hand wearily tries to keep her chin from falling to her chest. A side-glance is all her exhausted body and mind can muster for Erik — the demands of business can drain even the toughest person. She quietly explains how the stresses of her job, like the papers on her desk, are rising uncontrollably. Erik hugs her and brings a smile back to her face all the same.

I stand beside Mike, who looks like he is losing steam. After working the kinks out of a passenger's neck, I turn to him and ask him how he is feeling.

"Connecting with these strangers is incredibly energizing. I wish I had more to give!" Mike answers.

I pause before I answer, thinking about the next two days.

"Mike you've done the work of a hundred!" I tell him, and he has. "The real story of the weekend is the way in which you have been a catalyst for all that has and is about to happen!" From the free hotel rooms, gym passes, and countless volunteer arrangements, Mike has more than stepped up to the plate — he's hit a home run!

Across town we are carted to an arena where the local team, the Thunder Wolves, will battle their cross-country rivals from Medicine Hat. Inside, the cold air chills in our throats as if we've just sucked breath mints. The arena begins to fill with fans who jostle for comfortable positions on the bleachers.

Mike has the bird's eye view of the game, recording it from the commentators' box. He introduces us to the announcers then funnels us into a room where our volunteer duties for the evening are outlined. Plastic garbage cans overflowing with hockey pucks crowd the room. I secretly wonder if we've been sent here to polish the pucks for the next practice. Knowing that hockey is religion in Canada, it wouldn't surprise me.

The volunteer coordinator comes into the room and tells us that we've been enlisted as the primary sales force — we'll sell pucks for a dollar during the Chuck-a-Puck fundraiser for the hockey club. At half time a truck will be rolled out onto centre ice and 2,000 potential Cy

Young award winners will hurl their sponge pucks at the truck, hoping to land one in the cab. All of this will take place between the second and third period, so we have about 40 minutes to put a puck in the palm of everyone in attendance. The math seems impossible; we need to sell 50 pucks a minute to put one in every hand. Using the expertise honed by promoting kindness across the country, we are confident we can convince these diehard fans to support the home team. We organize ourselves two by two and enter the crowd hawking our wares as if we are selling peanuts at a Yankees game.

"Pucks! Get yerrr pucks! Red hot and going quick!" Brad bellows to the crowds.

"Only a buck a puck gets you a brand-new car! Just land your puck in the cab of the truck and win!" Erik shouts from the other end of the arena while bounding up and down stairs like a gazelle on a game reserve. "These pucks could, should, and will change the very course of your life. Come on, take a risk! Make this an adventure. This could be the TSN turning point of your life!"

"I'll even throw in a free massage!" Brad yells from ice level, facing a section of 200 hockey fans (197 of whom are men).

I wish I had the confidence of these two sales pros. I'm bent on "faking it 'til I make it" and it starts to work. I see a steady increase in revenue from the first to second period.

Val takes a more cautious approach, explaining the value of contributing to the Thunder Wolves Hockey Program. "Every single dollar donated makes a difference.

Your dollars will ensure that these men will achieve both their physical and educational goals. You are investing in a program that will make a difference in the lives of youths for years to come."

Teens try to keep up with Erik and Brad, pleading to be a part of the Kindness Crew for the night. Erik obliges, enlisting the young sales associates to help meet his sales goal. Meanwhile, his entrepreneurial genius has allowed him to open up a totally new market: the visiting team. Erik marches straight to the penalty box where a daunting six-foot-six bruiser from the Medicine Hat team is taking his punishment. Erik extends his sympathy to the player in the box and offers him a hug. The player apparently can't hear Erik, but stands up and begins to yell. He motions for Erik to join him in the penalty box, but luckily the buzzer sounds. Erik is saved by the bell, but no sale is made.

A bellowing roar swirls around the building, a whirlpool, funnelling the cheers of fans down onto the ice. The announcer raises his hand and signals for the crowd to shoot. It is man against machine, the odds brutally stacked in the fans' favour, 2,000 to one. They take aim and fire into the arena, trying to land their ammunition inside the vehicle. Hands launch continuous rounds from the bleachers, but the truck is resilient, repelling the sponge pucks as if protected by a force field. Those pucks that have made it inside the cab will be put into a draw at the end of the season. The rink gates open and a flood of kids race to clean up the carnage, using hockey sticks instead of brooms, sweeping the pucks back into the buckets.

Exhausted, we adjourn for the night knowing that Mike will certainly have the slate filled for tomorrow.

The next day Mike has arranged an act of kindness that will test our culinary skills and put us in charge of cooking for more than a hundred of the homeless in the community at a local soup kitchen. He hopes the act of kindness will extend not only to the people who use the soup kitchen but also to the volunteers who work assiduously day after day.

Inside the kitchen, Erik's years of restaurant experience make him a natural leader for the task. We fall in.

"Chris, go down to the food storage under the building and see what canned items are still available. Brad, I'll need you to cut up these vegetables. I need the carrots in circles and potatoes diced. Val, put that pot on the element!"

Erik's voice is rushed for a reason. With only two hours to prepare a meal for a 100, all on board will need to pull their weight. The kitchens he normally is in charge of would have 10 times the resources. These are minor hurdles to Erik and he pushes ahead.

In the basement we search for the ingredients needed for Erik's creation. Wall to wall, floor to ceiling, are shelves filled with canned goods containing every imaginable vegetable or fruit. We marvel at the variety, given the green light to take whatever we want. All of the food in the pantry has been donated from farmers, families, and businesses in the community. The vast supply is another reminder of the invisible hands that have helped to sustain the organization.

Back in the kitchen Erik continues to command the group, "Chop this, dice that, mash these, and cook those!" Cans of corn pop like champagne bottles, casserole dishes are placed on the counter, and once the ingredients are layered, Erik lifts his concoction into the oven. An hour later we stand, aprons in hand, amazed by the artistry and organization of Erik's culinary feat.

The supper crowd starts to file in as we take off our aprons. We want to wait and find out how our food is received, but we leave the pans in the oven for the staff to serve. The oven doors open and release the warm smell of a chicken casserole that has been baking for over an hour. A few of the regulars make their way to the kitchen window offering a smile and friendly conversation before dinner.

We are told that the crowds are a cross-section of virtually every class: teenagers, former college students, fathers, mothers, and professionals. Most of these people at one time had a stable life — family, homes, careers — but for many just one wrong turn, one bad day has forced them to rely on the generosity of strangers. This type of life is not a choice for most. I am reminded of all that we take for granted living in Canada, of the luxuries most of us have grown accustomed to. I can't help but think that we could easily have fallen into the same trouble. The experience is an invaluable reminder of the necessity of charity in a community. We are all in need, though it manifests itself in different ways.

Before we leave, two tall gentlemen dressed in pressed black suits walk through the door, their hands gripping trays filled with individually wrapped chocolates, specialty cheeses, and a medley of vegetables. I assume they are from a catering company with excess supplies.

"These food trays are from my mother's funeral service. Today, after the service, I just kept thinking about the way she lived her life. She cared for others all the time and I know she would want to make sure that this food does not go to waste. Mom would want it to help someone else. Can you use it?"

"Of course! Thank you so much," I answer and place the trays out for people to enjoy before dinner.

His thoughtfulness in a time of personal tragedy is further evidence that the good in this community could outshine the bad. People, like this man, like Mike, ensure that the community grows stronger, that acts of kindness, no matter how big or small, are never wasted.

We slip out the door, allowing the regular volunteers to serve the food. We have worked one night while their regular volunteers have worked hundreds.

Mike sees us off, thanking us for coming to his hometown to help. I feel indebted to him for orchestrating this

The Crew honour a kindred spirit at the Terry Fox Memorial in Thunder Bay.

entire weekend, and for reminding us that one person can make a difference. We have had each other for constant support and reassurance; Mike has had to go it alone. His strength and commitment will continue to guide us for the rest of our journey.

On the edge of town we stop to look at the statue of Terry Fox. He is a true Canadian hero, someone who in the end gave his life for what he believed in. Though his run ended here, the real journey, his mission to help, lives on in the millions who take part in the annual Marathon of Hope to raise money and awareness for cancer research. Certainly living in the shadow of this statue has helped guide Mike and many others to harness hope for change.

TORONTO — CHRIS

After a night sleeping in the motorhome under the dancing northern lights, and hours on the highway, we navigate the tributaries of Toronto. The bus floats into the city like a tugboat upriver, weaving through four-lane-wide highways, honking cars, and sudden on-ramps. There is a feeling of excitement, increased banter, and we crowd the front of the bus for a view of the famed Toronto: Chinatown, Little Italy; the Skydome, the CN Tower; and of course that eternal landmark for the youth of Canada — MuchMusic!

The CN Tower pokes through the fog that blankets the city. At last, the veil will be lifted and we will have a chance to see "the centre of the universe." People scoff when they hear we'll be hugging people on the streets of Toronto: "Good luck," "You'll have a tough time," "You might get an unexpected surprise (a gestured punch!)." We expect healthy scepticism; we've learned that's par for the course. Tomorrow, we'll take our chances. Our mark will have to made face to face, one person at a time. A city this big is intimidating though, and I secretly wonder what difference we will be able to make.

At 4:00 a.m. I awake to the throbbing sound of the alarm. It doesn't comfort me to know that it is 1:00 a.m. back home. Minutes later Jonathon begins to corral our crew. He pounds on my door yelling, "We have to be at Breakfast Television's studios in an hour — get a move on!"

The Crew stands for kindness at a Raptors game.

If only I had the energy to respond. If only I had the motivation to be on television at six in the morning. I remind myself of our mission, and the market that we are in — there'll by thousands watching this program and hopefully some of them will take up the challenge.

Our publicist, Lorraine, flown in from B.C. to help us manage media and requests, enthusiastically runs down the day's schedule. "First, we've got Breakfast TV, then a few radio interviews, downtown to launch the Volunteer Day at SAS Canada's headquarters on Yonge Street. Then to the National Ballet. We are working on Global television and CBC. The hotel will be offering a free Thanksgiving dinner on Monday. It looks like the Queen is leaving town today, so I wouldn't expect too much media!"

At Breakfast TV we indulge in coconut doughnuts and cinnamon bagels — sugar makes for talkative guests. Erik has four bagels, Brad sips black syrup (two creams, six sugars), but I know caffeine will do nothing for my stage fright. Val is waiting in the corner, meeting the bands (rap and reggae are on the breakfast menu today) and getting directions to the backdoor clubs and cafés in the city core.

"All I've seen of the Toronto nightlife is Electric Circus on TV. I want the real thing — something out of the way, house beats blaring, a few hundred people . . ." Val says, hoping for the inside scoop.

"A minute-thirty to kindness!" the cameraman shouts. "Use the stools from the coffee bar. I want the tall one by the host, the rest at an angle facing him. We're cutting in after weather. Five, four . . ."

"Welcome back to Breakfast Television. Today in the studio we have four young men from Victoria who are on a mission to brighten your day. I'm joined by Chris, Erik, Val, and Brad of The Extreme Random Acts of Kindness Tour . . . The Extreme Crew . . . The Random . . ."

"The Extreme Kindness Tour," Brad interjects.

"Thank you. So, you're nice guys here to do nice things in Toronto. I think this is just what Toronto needs! You also have a challenge for the city: commit at least one act of kindness today. Maybe you can help out our viewers, give us some examples of what people can do?"

Erik leans forward. "It's simple. Pay for someone's coffee, go down to the SPCA and walk a dog, bring blankets to a shelter, take your friend surfing! Or, let us do

The Kindness Crew in a media scrum — let the tour begin!

The Crew posing in front of their home-away-from-home.

Random dance lessons from the master of moves, Brad Stokes, in Calgary.

Brad shows all the signs of a kindness protester in Edmonton.

Chris adds to the local colour at a Roughriders football game in Regina.

Chris makes others glad with gladiolas.

Erik makes friends with a piano prodigy at the local hospital.

Chris delivering pretzels and a bud with a Kindness recruit in Kitchener.

Val and Chris falling for Niagara.

Kitchener boasts one of the largest Oktoberfests and the smallest leiderhosen. Just ask Erik!

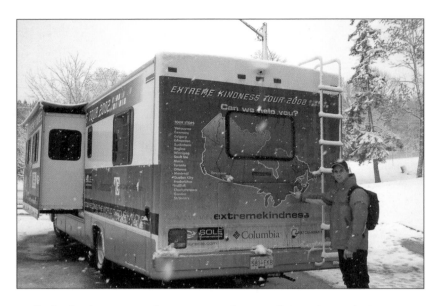

Erik checks the map and current weather conditions in Fredericton.

Hats off to Brad who nails the spa experience in Halifax!

Recycling kindness can be a good start!

Erik in a moment of meditation before meeting the Premier proudly sports the gear of champions in P.E.I.

Kindness around the globe — be a part of it!

Erik has his hands full with kindness.

something for you. You have four healthy helpers at your beck and call. Just email, fax, write, or call the station and we'll be there."

The interview continues and Toronto responds to our challenge: a single woman needs help moving, a school wants us to visit, a turkey needs serving on Thanksgiving, a stylist wants to cut our hair! Close to a hundred in all, and only four of us, one motorhome, and three days! We might get to half. But Erik screams no! We must at least try to tend to all of them — how else are we supposed to make a splash, make a real difference! This is the Extreme Kindness Tour — we have to take it to the next level. We all agree to try, but one act at a time!

Downtown skyscrapers tower over us like cement trees, shading the streets. Our campaign will start from the sky on the 16th floor of the sas head office. First, we swarm the employees on the first floor, giving group hugs to suits stuck in elevators, demanding that janitors quit their jobs (for an hour) to let us do the cleaning, and bounding over desks to massage the tired shoulders of secretaries.

We speed up the elevator shaft to a press room crowded with cameras and crazed eight year olds who have sworn their allegiance to the Kindness Crew — at least for the day. Mrs. Smith explains that these 20 students have been following the tour — reading journals, watching videos, and putting compassion into action in their own school. They will be joining us in our attempt to prove to the people of Toronto that kindness is crucial. sas has sweetened the day with enough candy for every citizen in sight! You are not supposed to take candy from strangers, but with adult supervision, the kids will *give* candy to strangers!

Our press conference is more like a Tony Robbins workshop than an address to the media — interaction and energy are required of all in attendance! People need to experience the joy of being kind if they are to embrace this mission. Brad has everyone close his/her eyes and imagine the ripple effect of each act of kindness performed that day.

The microphone is passed to our sponsor, SAS, which has taken the challenge seriously and made it part of its business mandate. Karl Farrell, the president of SAS Canada, addresses the audience, revealing the initiative to both the media and the employees.

"Our company is inspired by the example that the Extreme Kindness Crew has set. SAS will now give each employee one day per quarter paid leave to perform random acts of kindness. SAS wants to foster a spirit of volunteerism and community involvement. This is a perfect fit for our business!"

There is applause from the audience (and a few high-fives from the staff) and the four of us turn to each other with looks of astonishment. This is a bold move toward corporate social responsibility.

Brad can't contain his enthusiasm. "SAS Canada has offices across the country. What an opportunity!"

"This is what we always hoped would happen. We have finally infiltrated the corporate sector!" Erik replies.

Val smiles and says, "This could be the catalyst that

other companies need, to recognize the value of volunteerism in the workplace. This could have a ripple effect right across the country!"

"No more time for talk!" Erik reminds us. "Let's hit the streets!"

Out on Yonge Street, each child is handed a fluorescent poster to get the attention of pedestrians. In writing that could be seen a block away, the signs read: EMAIL ME AND I'LL SCRUB YOUR TOILET! HONK IF YOU ARE KIND! Brad deputizes the new recruits. "You are now part of the Kindness Crew and you have a duty to your city, to your country. You must make as much noise as possible to alert everyone that today is a day of random kindness. You must ensure that no one, *no one*, gets by without a spoonful of kindness — feed it to them! People are hungry for something, but they don't know what. Go give it to them! Get out there and spread the word! Move it! Move it!"

It's as if the bell has just rung for recess. The first victim of their generosity is a busload of tourists from France. They are unloading single-file when a swarm of four-footers surround them. The translator tries to explain that this is normal and that the children of Toronto want to wish them a good day. Hugs and candy break the language barrier despite the odd confused question, *"Je ne comprend pas? Qu'est-ce que c'est? Les enfants. . . ."* Soon there is laughter and the flash of cameras — these short ambassadors have convinced them to adopt a new custom in a strange land.

The kids team up with our Kindness Crew and together

*Brad training the new recruits to be happy campers for
Toronto's Kindness Protest.*

we make sure that all who pass are complimented, given
a sugar rush, or are high-fived. Two of the SAS staff holding posters weave through the traffic at the stoplights,
encouraging drivers to honk for kindness. The answer is
a resounding yes, and the noon air fills with the howling
of a hundred horns alerting the entire block. It pulls
workers from their desks and soon noses are pressed
against glass as employees in the local office towers pine
for a chance to leave their cubicles and take part in the
madness. The spirit of the event captivates many, including the street vendors. One offers free hot dogs to those
brave enough to partake in the cause.

Midway through our on-the-street antics, word arrives
that royalty is right around the corner. Children in tow,

we make a break for the Queen's entourage. We are within 15 feet of the Queen's tightly guarded motorcade when she steps from the front doors of the hotel. Unfortunately, with only a few turns of the wrist and a few ta, tas she ducks into her Mercedes. I feel it is only fair that we treat the Brits with the same affection as the French, so I offer to hug one of the Queen's advisors about to get into her limo.

"Miss, don't leave without a goodbye hug!" I say to a woman in high heels and a tight grey suit.

"Now why would I do a thing like that?" she replies.

"Why not? Have you had a hug today? Better yet, have you been hugged by a *Canuck* today?"

"It all sounds wonderful young man, but I really must be going. The Queen has already left," she replies and ducks her head into the limousine.

I wave goodbye and attempt to move onto the next car. A stern police officer blocks my path — it seems I have gone far enough. Without hesitation, I turn to the officer and tell him *he* needs a hug. Before he has time to reply, I've got him. He blushes and his partners can't help but chuckle.

Undaunted by our brush (off) with royalty we push on.

The end of the day nears and we are all approaching burnout. At 4:00 p.m. we are entering our 12th hour of kindness. The work has been harder than we thought. Toronto and its citizens seem to stop for no one, especially in the business district. However, if there is one thing that could grab people's attention here it is the lure of money. Val reminded me I had a $100 bill wedged

Val leads the troops to the kindness barricades — take no prisoners!

between the leather folds of my wallet.

"Chris, why don't we use the money you were given last week?"

Prior to our stop in Toronto, we had been speaking to a group of Rotarians. After we spoke, a gentleman approached me and offered to donate $100 to the tour. I was taken aback by his kindness and explained to him that we were fortunate enough to have sponsors for the tour and we, personally, did not need his donation. He must have been a salesmen in his former life, for he wouldn't take no for an answer!

"If you don't need it, surely you can find someone else who does."

I accepted the money graciously, with a promise to

find an imaginative way to spend it.

We would pay forward his generosity on the streets of Toronto. We would turn this $100 into 100 smiles. The possibilities were endless. With the video camera in tow, we begin to interview every suit, student, and postal worker who passes. Each interview yields a new and creative way to dispense our dollars.

First we pose the question: What would you do if someone gave you $100, but you had to spend it on other people? The answers were as varied as the people we interviewed:

"I'd buy lunch for all of the homeless that I walk by every day."

"I'd donate the money to the Cancer research!"

"I'd pay for all the kids on Yonge Street to play video games."

"I'd buy presents for people, and give them an early Christmas."

"I'd use it to fund a documentary about the less fortunate."

"I think we should take this bill to the bank and break it into 100 loonies!" suggest four girls in unison.

Together, we trudge two blocks to the nearest bank and ask for change. A bewildered bank clerk obliges. Brad, the on-tour accountant, handles the money and once outside he doles it out — 10 crew members at 10 loonies each.

"We need to make sure this touches as many people as possible. Let's see how far we can stretch the money. Can we turn these coins into something else? Be creative," Erik says.

One dollar doesn't buy you much on the streets of Toronto — unless you know how to haggle (in the kindest possible way of course)! The four teenage girls who had joined our team take their loonies into a local pizza parlour and with a little bartering are able to bring the price of pizza down to a buck! The next person to walk in the door would be the first to taste their kindness.

"Why pay, when you can have it for free?" the girls asked in unison.

"Thanks! Is this on the up and up?" the gentlemen replies.

"Only if you do what the girls say and pay it forward!" the cook shouts from behind the counter.

"No problem, I'll leave a surprise on my co-worker's desk today when I get back to the office."

The spending continues: in a clothing store a shopkeeper decides that a dollar is good enough for a designer T-shirt. Erik decides that to be fair he would give the shirt to the first person he met when he walked out the front door. A young skateboarder cruises by and Erik takes off after him.

"Hey, I'm giving away a shirt. Are you interested?"

The skater stops, and approaches Erik. "What's the catch dude?"

"Nothing, the shop gave it to me for a buck and I want to make your day! Just promise to pay it forward," Erik replies.

"Sweet! No problem."

We are only a block away from the MuchMusic TV studios and the girls decide to up the ante and involve a MuchMusic host.

Once we are on the studio doorstep, the girls press their faces against the glass and begin knocking furiously. Erik spots George Stroumboulopoulos, the heavy hitter of the hard rock scene at MuchMusic, across the road, and yells to alert the girls.

They surround him and George is quick to offer his support. The girls, with George in tow, boldly negotiate some bargain basement prices for coffee — a buck a cup — from a vendor.

George approaches two homeless teens sitting on a piece of cardboard and offers them a cup of coffee. A smile and a thank you are offered in return.

George says, "There are a couple of ways you can live life. You can ignore the people around you or not. I am not going to do that. I don't know how to do that. So if you don't ignore people, they are part of your world and you are a part of theirs. I believe that everybody is one bad day a way from needing something. Just one day!"

A cardboard sign lies between the teens that reads: TO GIVE IS GOOD KARMA. Looking down at the sign, Val says, "I could use some of that. How much will two dollars get me?"

At the end of the day, one thoughtful gift from a gentlemen in a community miles away funded an afternoon adventure on the streets of Toronto. His generosity has crossed the province and spread throughout a city.

GUELPH — VAL When we collapse in the
motorhome that night, we
check our email and discover
one from Colleen, a single mother writing from a shelter
for battered women. She asks if we can visit to cheer up
her children. Colleen describes how she and her daughters have spent the past seven months in the shelter —
both girls had spent their birthdays there and neither
had a party, not even a slice of cake. Her daughters have
become withdrawn and she is convinced we are the Crew
to give them a lift. Could we visit them in their new
apartment in Guelph?

My Ontario geography is not stellar, but I know
enough to know that this is not a scheduled stop. I grab
my daytimer and flip to a map of Canada. Ontario is the
size of a loonie and Guelph doesn't appear anywhere. I
need a better map. In the back of the motorhome we had
posted a giant map of Canada. We gaze at it every few days
with satisfaction, arms crossed, surveying the country,
marvelling at how far we have come. I beeline for the map,
flick on the light, and kneel on the bed, my face just inches
away from Canada's capital. I trace a reverse route with my
index finger from Ottawa to Toronto, hoping to find
Guelph somewhere along the way. No such luck: visiting
Colleen means backtracking and we are going "hell bent
for leather" in the other direction.

We have boasted that our tour was a choose-your-own-
adventure — we have a route, but if you want us to visit
we'll do our best to get there. Bathurst Inlet in Nunavut
was pushing it, but a place like Guelph certainly sounded

West to Guelph or North to Ottawa?

reasonable. The problem at the moment was that our schedule was especially tight and Ottawa was expecting us.

Brad, who was brought up by a single mother and knew how tough it can be, hangs his head.

Chris massages his temples and says after a pause, "I don't know how it can be done. That'd mean showing up a day late in Ottawa. We can't break our commitments on such short notice."

I would have to phone Colleen and tell her we couldn't make it. After a few rings the answering machine kicks in. "Machine," I whisper nervously to the guys who all nod, waiting to hear what I'll say. Erik pats my shoulder.

"Hey," an energetic voice begins, "you've reached Colleen, Rebecca, and Tess." Each said her own name, then, in unison, "Leave a message!" *Beeeep.*

"Hi Colleen, this is Val from Extreme Kindness." I picture Colleen and the girls arriving home, seeing the flashing red light on their machine. "Ahhh, how ya doin'?" I falter. The guys look at me. I have been the go-to guy for some of the biggest interviews on the tour and now I was choking on an answering machine with an audience of three. "We're just phoning to say that we can't wait to see you! We'll be there tomorrow, about two-ish!" I hang up the phone quickly and don't say anything. It was reckless, irresponsible, impulsive, and totally the right thing to do. "Sorry, guys, but I couldn't say no. I couldn't do it."

They look stunned. I have just made our next few days infinitely more complicated. We will have to phone Ottawa and beg to reschedule events and interviews.

"We could drive through the night!" Erik erupts. Erik's ideas often come suddenly and at high volume. The thought hadn't occurred to any of us. It was actually a stroke of genius: we'd arrive a little road-weary at the next stop, but we wouldn't let down Colleen and her girls.

On our way to Guelph we pick up a few props: pumpkins for the girls to carve (Brad's idea); canned pumpkin, brown sugar, pie shells, butter, and cinnamon (Erik "Iron Chef" Hanson's idea); fruits and veggies (Chris "Where's the Carbs?" Bratseth's idea); and chocolate (my high-cal solution to everything). Erik prepares a hamper of jackets, shirts, gloves, scarves, toques, and winter shoes from Columbia Sportswear. We are ready.

Colleen's building neighbours a park bursting with the burnt reds, dusty yellows, and rusted oranges of late autumn. The whole town smells of October; gusts carry the smoky smell of burning leaves, tickling our noses.

We make our way to the door of Colleen's apartment. I wedge three large pumpkins between me and the wall to free a hand to knock. I hear a giggle and scurrying inside, then Colleen's voice saying, "Go on, they're your guests. They've come a long way to visit you — it's up to you to welcome them." I hear embarrassed teenage laughter as the door opens.

Tess is standing in front of her mother, rolling her eyes and trying to look casual, but she can't pull it off. She bursts into laughter and runs into the next room.

"Hi, I'm Colleen," says our blushing host, extending a hand.

"There'll be none of that," says Chris, gripping Colleen in a bear hug. She claps her hands when Chris put her down — she is ready for her next hug. We place our hampers on the floor. Their new apartment is spacious, but bare. There is a couch and one chair in the living room, packing crates form a coffee table, and a lamp sits on the floor in the corner.

"I'm so happy, so grateful, you boys could come. The girls have already changed since I told them you were coming. Tess, my youngest, she's 13, has been bouncing around all day. I keep telling her she'll disturb the neighbours and that we'll get kicked out before we move in. Rebecca should be here in a few minutes. I thought I'd make some tea. I don't have any milk so it'll have to be black."

Colleen is radiant and — it seems — amazed that her

email has summoned a band of roaming do-gooders. She looks middle aged and wears a grey wool sweater with sleeves that bunch up slightly at the wrists. Thick blond hair is swept back from a face framed by a pair of steel-rimmed glasses. Though Colleen is happy to see us, she also seems awkward and we feel odd sitting on her couch as she makes tea.

There have been times during the tour when we have been taken aback by how difficult some people find it being recipients of kindness, even though those same people have *asked* us for help. Whenever we encounter this we try to show them — sometimes overtly though more often covertly — that they are helping us too.

On the pretence of assisting in the kitchen, Brad strikes up conversation. After some small talk he mentions that he has been raised by a single mother and never knew his dad. The tea does not emerge from the kitchen for 20 minutes.

We can hear everything in the next room. Brad explains that, being raised by women, he suffered from "estrogen overload," wedged between his mom and his sister. Being the only man in a house of alpha-females as a young 13 year old "was brutal." Colleen emits a muffled laugh; she must have a sleeved hand over her mouth.

The rest of the story is interrupted by Chris and Erik's giggling when Tess comes running down the hall practically in hysterics, "Mom, Chris and Erik are using all my hair stuff; they look like girls!"

We are waiting for the fashion show and sipping our first cup of tea when Rebecca walks in. If Tess is the spitting image of her blond, blue-eyed mother then Rebecca is the exact opposite. At 16, she is dressed head to toe in black, with short, spiky, jet black hair, a ring through her lower lip, her fingers heavy with silverware. I brace myself.

Rebecca stands completely still, eyes wide, and raises her arm in a windmill wave hello. We all get up from the couch and smother her in typical Kindness Crew fashion. When the dust clears, Rebecca walks over to her mom and sits on her lap.

"They're not usually like this; this is incredible. After we left my husband, they shut themselves off. They were very worried about me those last couple months of my marriage, but now they're goofing around," Colleen blurts, adjusting a few stray strands of hair.

"Well, *we* haven't done anything," I venture.

Rebecca locates the chocolate immediately, picks through Erik's box and finds a shirt, then pulls it over her head, being careful not to catch it on any of her piercings.

"Whaddya think, Mom?"

Colleen makes a frame with her two hands and looks at Rebecca through it, "I think I like you in orange, or any colour for that matter."

Tess walks into the living room and waves her arms to make an announcement. "I'd like, I'd like . . ." she begins then leans back to look down the hall — Erik is prompting her. She nods and whispers, "OK." She begins again, "I'd like to introduce the new fall line: this is how women are wearing their hair this autumn . . . it's sassy and chic!"

Erik and Chris appear with Kelly and camera in tow. They have raided the girls' stash of cosmetics, from pink berets to plastic coloured bangles. Tess can't control herself.

"Kelly, turn off the camera, you're wasting film," Brad laughs. The rest of us coo appropriately at the labour-intensive hair. Erik prances by the couch, twisting a curl of hair.

"How long did you have to sleep on it to get your hair like that, Erik?" Dave pretends to be from *Vogue* magazine, "Seriously?" Rebecca and Tess like Dave's question and giggle in anticipation of Erik's campy response.

I look over at Colleen. Her eyes are glistening — this may be better than any birthday present money could buy.

LONDON — BRAD

People expect us to be more than ordinary men. Our *goal* is extraordinary but *we* are not and today is a perfect example. We're late. Lindsay, Marie, and Sara have been waiting for us on the Western University campus to join the Crew for a cleaning marathon; you show us the dorm, we'll make it over. The girls are expecting something a bit more glamorous so I whip out the camera to take it up a notch. I tell them about visiting the Columbia Sportswear factory across town the day before and delivering hugs to employees via a forklift of kindness. It's not always *what* you do but *how* you do it. In Kitchener that day, Erik donned a pair of lederhosen, in the spirit of Oktobefest, and danced in the street to accompany an accordion player.

On our way to "the messiest room" in the dorms we

are stopped by an authoritative voice that demands, "Who are you and why are you filming in here? You do know that you need a permit to use that, don't you?" The authoritative voice belongs to Ted, the resident don.

During our adventures, rules and regulations have required some quick thinking. Generally, our tactic has been to remain friendly and apologize for not asking permission, and to assure the officials we meant no transgression. This is not working so well today. Ted informs us that we can come back next week and he will obtain a filming permit for us. I tell him we'll be miles away in our huge blue motorhome, parked out front. Ted asks if we have a parking permit. If not, it must be moved in the next half hour. We manage to buy a bit of time and promise to be in and out before he can call the authorities.

In room 303 Sanjay appears, eyeglasses ajar, yellow baseball cap tilted and a puzzled look on his face.

"We're the Kindness Crew and we're here to clean your room. Brad will keep you company, the girls are going to clean your laundry, I'll do the dishes, Chris will empty the trash, Val will organize your desk, and Ted will clear out your closet," Erik orders.

In no time the closet is neatly organized and the clothes categorized. A disco ball hangs from the ceiling above a desk perfectly readied for study and homework. Val has even found some balloons and coloured light bulbs to set the mood. This room has had an "Extreme makeover." Sanjay is shaking his head — he can't quite convince himself that 20 minutes has made this difference. Our job finished, we say our goodbyes and drive away before campus security decides to tow our B.C. bus straight to the impound. London might have been a short stop, but we sure cleaned up this town.

SARNIA — BRAD

I do not believe that going to Sarnia is a good idea; it is out of our way. The motorhome is fairly banged up due to extensive travel, the windshield wipers are not working properly, and the interior power is all but gone. We have a mountain of accounting, editing, and writing to do and I'm hungry, tired, and need a hot shower.

Cold air and thick fog make islands of buildings as we pull up to the Holiday Inn. Our local contact, Rod, has kept the kitchen open for us. I like Rod; I like him a lot. Rod is a lawyer, a town councillor, and a Rotarian, and he is personally picking up the tab for the next three days. His friend Terry, who owns a flower shop in town, will be donating some 300 flowers tomorrow. We are speaking to the Rotarians over breakfast, then we have an interview with the local newspaper, we meet the mayor, and then speak at a town council meeting. We will also visit several schools and greet American tourists as they travel over the border.

Rod listens to our tales of adventure and success and I am calmed by his fatherly presence. Sometimes the best act of kindness is just listening. Often people in conversation don't listen so much as wait to speak. To properly communicate it is critical to actually hear what is being said. This is applicable whether it be a father taking time to hear about his son's first day of school or a head of state listening to the concerns of other world leaders.

The next morning, I find myself speaking from a podium to 50 of Sarnia's most respected community members and leaders. A sea of ties, suits, and other business outfits stretch before me. I focus my discussion under four headings: kindness to the self, colleagues, clients, and community. I urge each Rotarian to first be kind to themselves in body, mind, and spirit, then to look for opportunities to perform acts of kindness for those they work with and for.

"You do not change completely the moment you walk into work. Your own personality and your goals can play a role in the office." I say this as someone who has been less than true to himself in past jobs. I end the speech with a discussion about giving to the community so that everyone profits.

An hour later we are at one of Sarnia's shopping centres and there are hundreds of people in need of lilies, roses, and daisies. We split up and approach mall patrons. Val's first catch comes from a trio of construction workers on their lunch break.

"You want to give me what? Do I look like a guy who wants a flower?"

"Come on, Bill, it will match your helmet."

"I don't want a rose, give me a lily instead."

Chris approaches two elderly women. "Ladies can I give you a flower today?"

One lady looks askance at him and rejects his offer. "What? No, I don't want to buy any flowers, thank you."

"No, Jean. I think the young man said they are free!"

"Tea?"

"No, free!"

Twenty minutes later the mall is a bouquet of smiling people and we are on our way.

Saying it with flowers in Sarnia.

During an interview the reporter asks us how we feel about being so close to the U.S.A., our original goal, and if we plan to do a similar tour in the States.

"Travelling across Canada has been a great way for us to understand what being Canadian is all about. We would love to go to the States, too, and have already begun laying some of the ground work," Chris beams.

Secretly I worry, despite Chris's confidence, that the next tour will never happen. It is still a long way off. The main roadblock is finding the time to secure sponsors and arrange accommodation, partnerships with community organizations, and media. We have more experience in event planning, public speaking, filming, and writing than we did a year ago, but finding sponsorship for another tour will be tricky. Ideally, the U.S. tour will be the next step on a tour that would take us around the world. Reaching out to other nations would be an accomplishment beyond my dreams.

That said, I wouldn't mind the occasional rest day if we're going to do this again. Four hours of sleep is just not cutting it.

The mayor's office has a formidable view of the city. Chris is sitting in the mayor's chair while Erik poses as his diligent secretary. God help the city of Sarnia. The real mayor is talking to Val, on camera, about the city's reputation for kindness. Sarnia is full of people who give to others and look out for their neighbours. He agrees to join us across the street as we barge into offices and boardrooms to dispense coffee and hugs. Before the day is through Rod offers some unexpected news: "I booked you an appointment with my mechanic. He'll fix the windshield wipers and your interior power at no cost."

The wipers will work perfectly and I will be able to see clearly again. All I needed was a little help.

OTTAWA — BRAD

I turn a corner and see a crowd of a hundred Delta hotel employees waiting outside in the cold waving banners and signs to welcome us. Cheers and whistles grow in volume as we park in front of the happy mob. I can do this: 100 people=100 hugs.

Inside, a buffet of food and even more people await us. We have no sponsor obligations until the press conference and ensuing Kindness Marathon tomorrow, then we will stop in at a hospice. It will be the first time since my mother passed away that I'll visit cancer patients.

This afternoon, Val has set up an hour-long interview and kindness event in the market square with Global TV. At a four-way intersection lined with outdoor stalls, we buy five large pumpkins and borrow some utensils from the Beaver Tail (flat doughnuts in the shape of a beaver tail) vendor. Unfortunately, Erik returns without chainsaws, axes, or swords, just spoons and a knife that can barely cut jam.

"They wouldn't let me play with anything sharp," Erik says gloomily.

Two of us will have mikes and will stay within 10 feet of the camera. The other two are kindness gophers drawing people into our circle. We are going to persuade people to carve a pumpkin and then give it to a stranger. Their work of art is paid forward when they give it away. Erik is armed with two dull and unpolished spoons and approaches a man in a black dress coat rushing across the intersection with umbrella in hand. The man does not slow down to hear Erik's pitch, but rather speed walks around this talking obstacle. Erik continues to chase him for a block. I hope he remembers we're only on air for an hour.

I approach a family of four, including a young brother and sister who surely will not be able to resist my offer. But resist they do. The young girl says something in French to her father and I begin an uncomfortable game of charades. After thoroughly embarrassing myself, the little boy says, "Why is he shouting, Papa?"

I feel profoundly stupid. The parents are trying very hard to not laugh at my red face. The children, quickly forgetting my odd behaviour, are rivetted by the sight of the huge Global TV camera. I lower my voice and speak at a normal volume. "Who wants to be on TV?"

Chris takes over for me and introduces the friendly Francophone family to most of central Canada. The brother and sister are intent on seeing who can grab the biggest fistful of seeds from the jack o' lantern. I step back and reflect on my first pre-Quebec French experience. Not speaking the language adds a new challenge.

"Ladies and gentlemen, the world championship of pumpkin carving has begun. Who has the courage to challenge our current champions?" Chris shouts.

No one seems inclined to step up to the plate. Erik has

been gone for almost 10 minutes and I have a vision of him in a business meeting challenging a group of suits to an extreme act of kindness. Before I have time to imagine Erik being taken away by security, he reappears with three teenagers. The two girls are given spoons while the young man takes a mouthful of pumpkin and spits it out onto the newspaper. I watch as a jack o' lantern is produced in less than five minutes with the use of only two hands and a healthy set of incisors.

"Ladies and gentlemen, I give you your Canadian pumpkin eating and carving champion!" Chris cries as the last bite is taken and the smiling teen holds his masterpiece above his head. His teeth are stained orange and bits of seed hang from his lips.

At the local hospice I am joined by over 20 Delta hotel employees in order to prepare tonight's dinner. I had thought hospices were always within hospital perimeters, but this one is also a shelter and soup kitchen. Apparently there is more to a hospice than providing comfort to the dying. We visit some of the hospice patients upstairs and I steel myself against the sight and sounds that are all too familiar. I am reminded of my mother's foggy stare, of the morphine stupor that rendered her "almost dead." It has taken me six months to get over the nightmare and I don't want to lose the strength I've gained, but I refuse to remain afraid of death.

Inside a small room we meet Pete, a man of about 50, who has a month to live. He has no family, but seems to find comfort in his friends on the floor, his books, and his memories. There are many others like Pete and the four of us spend the next hour keeping them company and listening to their stories.

I walk outside and stand in the sun, remembering my mother at her best. One of the last things she taught me was to never underestimate the power of a single gesture. Earlier today I was asked if one person, one act of kindness, can truly make a difference. Could it generate enough goodwill to circle the globe? People never question the destructiveness of a single man, but they find it impossible to believe that one man can connect the world through kindness. I know we will not change the world by ourselves, but I hope the four of us can do something positive. The domino effect is sure to multiply kindness if people believe in themselves as much as they do in others.

Create Your Own Kindness Protest

1. Create your own Kindness Crew!

This activity is perfect for a class project at a high school or as an active lunch break at a stressful office! The more the merrier, although you only need three or four people.

2. Buy or borrow the supplies for your signs.

You may need to buy supplies, but it can be done cheaply. Depending on the number of people taking part in the activity, you will want somewhere between 12 and 25 signs. Purchase some light wood at a lumber supplier. Or, for a free alternative, get your friends to use their hockey sticks as sign handles — this makes the protest clearly Canadian! Get some card stock (stiff paper) from a stationery store or, if you are at a school, ask the art department if it would be willing to donate some paper to the kind cause. You will probably want two pieces per sign so you can write on both the back and front.

3. Let the creative juices flow and design your signs.

Half the fun of the protest is creating the signs with your friends, the more outrageous the better! The idea behind the protest is to let pedestrians partake in a brief moment of fun and help spread the word, so make the signs funny. YOUR HAIR LOOKS GREAT TODAY! and DON'T FORGET TO PHONE YOUR MOTHER! are perfect.

Staple two pieces of your decorated card stock to each other, then slip the wooden handle (or hockey stick!) into the envelope you have created. Use your stapler to attach your paper envelope to the wood.

4. Hit the streets!

Find an intersection with lots of foot traffic and place an equal number of people on each corner. While pedestrians are waiting for the light to turn green, ask them if they would like to take part in the world's friendliest protest and carry a sign to one of your friends on the other side of the intersection. Encourage protesters to yell out what's written on their signs. Be respectful of people's boundaries; surprisingly, not everyone will want to participate. Also, be mindful of the traffic.

5. Spread the word!

Tell us your story by posting it on our Web site message board, extremekindness.com. Make a presentation with the signs, or even better, film it and show others who may want to join the Crew next time!

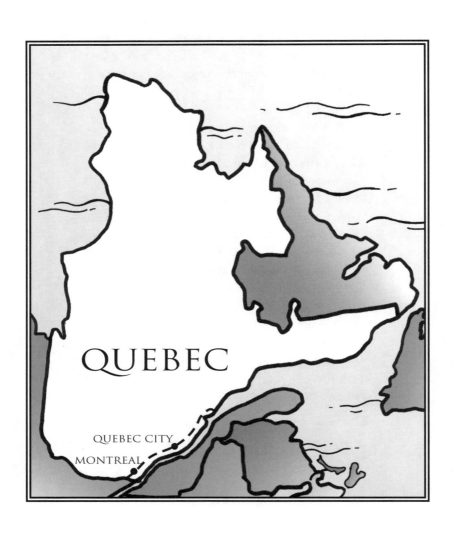

QUEBEC

QUEBEC CITY

MONTREAL

QUEBEC

Compassion is the basis of all morality.
— *Arthur Schopenhauer*

MONTREAL — VAL In Montreal everything has a little more, well, as the French say, *je ne sais quoi* — the food is more delicious, the people more sophisticated, and the music is just a little jazzier. You can't walk a block in Montreal without falling in love or stumbling across people carousing on a *terrasse*. Each of us has had the experience of opening our front door, hair everywhere, breath smelling like last night's garlic, wearing a tattered dressing gown, only to discover a beautiful visitor waiting on the doorstep. This is how we feel arriving in Montreal: we are confronted by a city and people so refined and full of culture our winter jackets turn to terry towel.

The hotel staff, from housekeepers to the head chef, are lying in wait just inside the foyer. Chefs in their crisp whites hold pewter trays piled high with hors d'oeuvres. The most flattering and unexpected surprise, though, is a poster with our faces plastered on it. The picture has been taken off the Web site and is a shot of us in the West Edmonton Mall. Smaller reproductions of the poster are framed in all the hotel elevators — *"Gentillesse Extrême!"*

After steering through the maze of balloons and platters of Montreal smoked beef we go up to our rooms and take in the lights of rue Sainte-Catherine, sidewalks thick with winter shoppers. The St. Lawrence glistens in the distance, boats floating ghostlike on its waters. Montreal's little countries are pulsing, too, in anticipation of the night. Chinatown has steam curling above its pagoda roofline, as if a thousand dim sum baskets have had their lids lifted at once. *Le Quartier Latin* is warming up, busy buffing its leather shoes in anticipation of tripping the light fantastic on the dance floor. Little Italy's fresco of Mussolini overlooks the warm *trattorias* and all seems right with the world.

I go to bed and dream of Canada's most vivid and extroverted city. But over the next several days I know it will be the people, not the cathedrals, cafés, or serpentine cobbles of *Vieux-Montréal* that will leave a lasting impression. Tomorrow, I promise myself, I will find the real Montreal.

The next morning at a soup kitchen I consider the stereotypes of the homeless perpetuated by the media: they are insane, drains on "the system," diseased, or high. Moving from small town to mega-metropolis, we are constantly reminded of the resolve, dignity, and intelligence of the denizens of the cold corners of urban Canada, but inside the kitchen the scene is bleak.

A man with thick, black, uncombed hair sits in the corner. He wears a bomber jacket with newspapers crumpled and stuffed into the lining for added warmth. When I ask him his name he smiles and says, "We don't have names." He winks and puts out his bowl to be refilled.

His words echo in my head as I ponder the myriad meanings of his response. He seems to suggest that he — like everyone else in the line — is anonymous. His reply seems to say, "We all look the same to you and you treat us all the same." His succinct answer is at the heart of what it means to be homeless. He hasn't just been denied shelter and warmth, but something much more precious — his identity — has been taken away by a system that inadequately supports him. Despite his circumstances, or perhaps because of them, he teaches me a valuable lesson and his manner is generous and gentle, without any trace of anger or bitterness. By most people's standards he has nothing to give, yet he still has everything. He is simultaneously the richest and most impoverished person I've ever had the pleasure of not meeting.

Sandy, a manager at the hotel, is especially moved by the visit. She gives people her full attention and reads between the lines, listening to what isn't said just as intently as what is. By the end of our stay Sandy's eyes are full of tears and she looks puzzled. I reach out and ask if she is OK.

"I had no clue, no idea people were struggling so hard

in *my* Montreal . . . living with so little."

Some approach the counter to stuff their pockets with packages of soda crackers. The thought of someone she now knows eating frozen soda crackers as an evening meal is almost too much for Sandy to bear.

"I have to come back here — we have to come back here — everyone from the hotel. We should do this more often."

Her choice of words, "*my* Montreal" impresses me immensely; if only more of us thought of the city we live in as ours, an offspring we have to love and care for like an extension of our own family. The anonymous faces that wander the streets are our neighbours, our brothers and sisters.

That afternoon we are in search of other ways to warm the hearts of Montrealers on a freezing October day. We want to do more than help the ubiquitous FedEx guy deliver packages, hold open heavy doors for grateful seniors, flog hot dogs, or give shoulder massages to stockbrokers as they wait for the walk signal. And then we find a project for which we can really bare our souls . . . well, maybe not our souls.

The McGill swim team is "stripping for loonies" (down to their Speedos and other spandex-inspired swimwear) to raise money for a swim competition in South Africa. Did I mention it was cold? The best part of the whole affair is that passersby aren't that impressed; it is well below zero and 40 young men in skin-tight neoprene are

In the swim of it — loonie antics while stripping for the McGill swim team fundraiser.

standing on the sidewalk but no one is taking pictures.

But perhaps it shouldn't surprise us. This is a little slice of Europe plunked right into the middle of Canada: both sophisticated and strange. It is a city where men dress as well as their wives and women leave contrails of perfume in their wake, a cosmopolitan city in which you can find Brazilian jazz at 4:00 am or satisfy a craving for shrimp burritos at breakfast, a place where you'll see business men and drag queens waiting casually at bus stops — totally beautiful, totally bizarre.

So pedestrians aren't that stunned with all the goose-bumpy flesh. *Vive le Quebec!*

I borrow the bullhorn that is hanging over the captain's shoulder and start to advertise. Apparently this is an annual event and the team will accept only loonies, nothing else. When a stranger throws them a buck, they gather their booty (pun intended) and tape the coins to the ground. The line of loonies is only a few paces long when we arrive, but once we announce that the world's first dry land synchronized swimming extravaganza is about to begin, the cash begins to pour in.

We jauntily fling knitted scarves around our necks like arctic Chippendale dancers and stride out onto the street during a red light. The swim team looks at us appreciatively, but seems happy that we have distanced ourselves from their troupe.

What follows can only be described as interpretative dance, though what was being interpreted is still unclear. I believe the most impressive part of our performance is when we plug our noses and wiggle to the ground, hands waving above us as we descend the imaginary depths. We butterfly, breaststroke, and dog-paddle the air, pirouetting and lunging as the mood dictates. It may be odd, but a small crowd gathers while Chris immitates the great Baryshnikov, chin high, tip-toes, back erect.

The swim team takes advantage of the newly captivated audience and gathers contributions. The line of taped loonies is growing so we bid the land-locked swimmers adieu and make our way past the huge pile of clothes heaped at the front gates at McGill University and move on to Radio CJAD.

CJAD is a sentimental visit for us because it had been the first station to phone us about the tour and the host of its late night show, Peter Anthony Holder, was the first person to break us in. Chris and I were in Victoria at the time and very nervous. To ease the pressure, we quickly scribbled quotes on pieces of paper in case we lost it during the live call. Chris and I spent the whole interview trying to sound casual, but were, in fact, reading verbatim perfectly crafted sound bites.

A woman named Alison had been in the late night audience during the first interview and was so intrigued by the interview that she phoned us the next day in Victoria, sparking a friendship that played out for months via email and phone. When our motorhome skidded to a stop in Montreal, one of the first things I did was phone her to see if we could meet for coffee or a meal. Now I was strolling through the chilly night air along Rue Roy, looking for the café where we had agreed to meet. When we did, it was as if we had known each other for years.

During our dinner, a man in the advanced stages of drunkenness wanders through the restaurant. Several waiters attempt to usher him out because he is disturbing tables and aggravating the patrons, but none of their attempts manage to calm or expel the man. So, in fine Montreal fashion, they pour him another drink. The logic seemed to be, "He won't leave, so let's pretend he's a customer and maybe nobody will notice." Of course, as fate would have it, he stumbles our way. He reaches out, grabs a fist of *frites* off my plate, stuffs them into his mouth, and stares at me, chewing. I ask him if he would like to join us. A french fry drops from his mouth.

The gentleman adjusts his jacket and thanks us, "*Oui, merci.* I would like vairee much to join you."

Alison stares at me, but all I can do is shrug. He makes

himself comfortable and introduces himself. It becomes immediately apparent that, in mixed company, the man could be polite, though far from sober, and when the waiter comes by he orders a bottle of wine for us "on my tab." A pleasant English-French dialogue ensues for about half an hour, at the end of which he takes his leave, thanking us for the conversation.

"Well that was . . . kind," says Alison with some irony.

"And odd," I add. "I've been brainwashed," I laugh. There had been moments during our marathons when people we approached had been aggressive, suspecting there was a catch. Nothing dissolved aggression, it seemed, better than a kind word or gentle behaviour. Perhaps the French translation of our name was more apropos: the Extremely Gentle Crew.

Our image as *gentle guys* had been interesting to monitor as we moved across Canada. It proved to be an uphill battle to disabuse the public of the notion that kindness equalled unmanly. The inherent stereotype assumed that young children and women were the sensitive, sympathetic ones, but we had to convince people that men suited the role too, that there is strength in kindness. Tonight, I had to put my money where my mouth was. In acquiescing to the man in the café, not submitting to his presence but honouring it, I had won him over, "killing him," as the expression goes, "with kindness."

On our last day in the city of smoked beef and bagels, we received an email from a local retirement home program coordinator saying there was a handful of seniors who would be "tickled pink" if we would go for a walk with them. Flattered by the email, we phoned back and insisted that the pleasure would be all ours.

Within a few hours we greet five seniors waiting on the curb for their field trip to the mall. The coordinator, Nancy, welcomes us and introduces us to the residents and the other support staff who'll join us.

Barry wears a tweed jacket and cap and doesn't say much; instead he prefers to clap. Chris, who must have been a flamenco dancer in a past life, connects with Barry instantly, clapping complex rhythms for his new acquaintances. Barry looks at Chris as if, after all these years, he has finally found someone who understands him. The deal is sealed: Chris will stick with Barry. Barry takes Chris' hand in his own.

Erik's job isn't quite as easy. A very brittle looking woman in a faux-fur black trench coat with a hood grabs Erik's arm with alarming vigour and asks, "Who are you?"

Erik smiles, amazed at her strength, and says, "I'm one of the guys that's walking with you today; we're all in this together!" Agnes, a mild agoraphobe, flips up her massive hood and makes her new walking partner disappear.

Eva is a charmer and by far the extrovert of the group. She wears a lime green Hermès silk scarf and matching green dress with polka dots. She has applied blush liberally to her cheeks and her accent is thick: "Vell all the hendsome men heff been taken, so I gezz it's you ant me!" She shuffles over to me with her walker, thrusting it in front of her as she goes, and takes a good look at me.

"Nice to meet you, Eva. My name is Val."

"If you're so nice then how come your name wasn't on my birthday card yesterday? Hmmm? Ha!" She says that she used to be a dancer and that's why she blows kisses all the time; she blows me several kisses on the bus and I am sitting right next her.

When we get to the mall Eva has no intention of pausing for a coffee break, taking off at breakneck speed shouting, "Let's lose the group!"

Nancy tells me that Eva is 92, and as far as she can tell, going as strong as when she arrived at the retirement home almost 10 years before. Eva is cutting high-speed deals with people as they pass, offering her walker for another man's cane, her scarf for another woman's purse. She finally hangs a right at the mall pharmacy and jerks her neck for me to follow her, and quick. She slips me a list and asks me to start reading.

I begin, "All right, we've got Kleenex (the yellow box not the blue), throat lozenges (butterscotch), lip balm (the one the pharmacist knows I like), Doritos. Does that sound right, Eva? Eva!"

While I was reading the list Eva had stolen another man's shopping cart while in the Skin Care aisle. The cart is in the way so she drops her walker and is now using the buggy. I quickly grab the walker and trot up to Eva, who is moving at a faster clip with the buggy's bigger wheels.

"Eva, you can't take that, he's going to notice it's missing, and," I kidded, "he'll come after you with the shaving cream."

"Iss OK," she says. "I heff the Kleenex by then." She

grabs her walker and shuffles around the corner. I return the shopping cart. The man is grateful but confused.

We manage to secure the other items without incident and the pharmacist is great with Eva, taking her mock abuse on the chin and getting her her special lip balm. The pharmacist pretends he keeps it behind the counter just for Eva, but winks at me and points surreptitiously to the lip balm in the Children's Suncare section: everyone has fun when Eva is around.

We hold open the mall doors as the seniors file out. Erik asks Agnes if she has had a good time. Agnes flips up her giant hood and keeps walking. Erik's face sags a little. Eva sees this and blows him a kiss.

QUEBEC CITY — CHRIS

The bus cruises quietly along the freeway, kicking up snow. Another season has turned, much quicker than we had expected. Our green thumbs are not used to being so far from the garden city of Victoria and are in danger of being blackened by frostbite in these frigid temperatures. There is a bright side to this cold day — the landscape glitters with the light of a million mirrors drenching the landscape with sunshine.

Inside the motorhome, Brad occupies the most dreaded spot in the bus: the driver's seat. When the vehicle was designed, the engineers intelligently intended to make it as efficient as possible. It was good on gas — only $280 to fill the tank — and there were large holes beside the gas pedals to ensure maximum uptake of air into the interior. Unfortunately, this means the driver's seat has a custom-made blow dryer set for "bone-chilling cold" that forces wind up into the driver's pantleg. We have stuffed socks, towels, and toilet paper into the holes to try to minimize the velocity of the air entering the bus. For added protection, Brad dons his snow survival suit: Gortex pants, jackets (two), wool and nylon gloves, a fleece toque, and a ball cap. His knee bounces up and down — subconsciously tapping S.O.S. — trying to keep warm.

"*Le rue de. . . .* How do you pronounce that?" Val shouts from the passenger seat, trying to direct us past the walls of Quebec City. Secretly he is hoping someone will take over navigation.

"Erik, your father was an elementary school French teacher. He must have imparted some of that knowledge to you!" Brad shouts.

"Ask Dave, he had the highest G.P.A. at university!" I say, hoping to deflect attention. I have a knack for getting the group lost in English and French.

Dave agrees to take the post. He loves to help navigate while penning updates for the tour Web site. His bird's-eye view of how the tour is progressing lets the country know 24/7 where we are and what we are doing. The front seat is the perfect place for him to do this: all he has to contend with there are his thoughts and the open road before him.

We arrive in La Ville de Quebec with just enough energy to gather our gear and stumble into the foyer of our hotel. We are led to the dining room where the general manager, Daniel, is waiting to welcome us. If we were travelling without the support of CHIP Hotels, we probably would be parking outside a Husky Station that night. More than the beauty of these buildings, it has been the warmth shown by those who work within them that has made our stops memorable. Many friendships have been formed in as little two days.

There are only two friendly faces at the table when we arrive (a small staff, considering the building is several stories high).

"We have a surprise for the four of you: a slight change of plans. We figured you would be exhausted from your work in Montreal so we've decided that this stop should be a chance for you to relax and recover from your months of hard work. We have a small event planned for tomorrow, but the rest of the time you are free to explore our beautiful city."

We are grateful for this opportunity to slow down and enjoy a café au lait, a warm bath, a walk through the old city, time to catch up on the writing that is always two days too late . . . but before I can make my own plans Erik has made some for me.

"What is the point of sitting around inside? Did you see this place? Throw on a pair of runners and let's jog the streets! It will be like running through the streets of Paris. The only way to really get to know a city is on foot!" he says with excitement.

"True, but usually walking is the preferred tempo and the streets are covered in snow and ice! I'm not sure if I brought my crampons," I reply, hoping that my humour will save me from having to brave the cold.

Somehow I'm talked into it and minutes later we are jogging down narrow roads, roads too narrow for vehicles. Cars struggle up the snow-covered, cobblestone lanes, wheels desperately trying to make it over each new hill. Erik's mission is to footprint every lane and we do our best. The city is a winter wonderland: chimneys fill the air with maple smoke while skaters pack the city's outdoor rink and shoppers visit stores in century-old buildings.

Near the end of the run, in a panting voice, I thank Erik for forcing me out of the hotel.

"Erik, I am so glad you made me come out here. I can't believe we are in our own country. This city is gorgeous!"

"I know — this is incredible! It feels like we are in Europe. I can't believe the tour has taken us this far away from our home."

After our dinner at the hotel, we make our way down the slippery sidewalks to a café for a night completely to ourselves, a night without the demands of filming. With the video camera tucked away in the hotel room, we can relax knowing that this night is just for us. The demands of travelling are taxing enough on their own, but to be on film and working every day has taken a toll that none of us could have expected.

At the café, we try to speak French to the waiter, but our tied tongues force us to stop after the first line. Collectively, *en français*, it seems we have the vocabulary of a three year old. We cowardly retreat to using hand gestures and head nods and a few hot drinks are negotiated.

Bird's-eye view of the breakfast buffet in Quebec City.

Laughter erupts as we recount memories of a tour that is only half finished.

One night's rest is all that is allowed and in the morning we set up a coffee and cake café (non-profit, of course) along with the hotel staff who have all taken the day to commit acts of kindness. An outdoor skating rink is behind us and skaters glide round an oval, while French carols sing from the speakers overhead. The Christmas spirit has come early to this part of Canada.

We all feel somewhat intimidated by the language barrier and are at a loss to translate. Hopefully, this won't create too much of a problem and a smile-and-hug will convey what we mean.

We receive some introductory French lessons before we strike off to meet the locals.

"Tell them you are *Gentillesse Extrême*," a reporter from *Le Soleil* advises. "I'm sure they'll have heard of you in the news." The phrase sounds like an oxymoron — gentle, but extreme. I hope and trust this introduction will work — it is all we've got!

A slow Sunday procession marches out of the churches and shops to our café — we're in business! Our café becomes a family affair and the children of the hotel staff join the marketing arm of the business, chasing down dozens of potential clients. The children are perplexed by our inability to communicate with the locals and our four-year-old friends take us one by one, hand-in-hand to recruit customers. Pedestrians are easily taken in by a breakfast offer from children. The adults, it seems, are more open to talking to a stranger if that person is a child. For most, a child still represents innocence and people have unfortunately lost much trust in other adults. Part of our mission today is to restore it.

The children remind us that kindness is fun, as each transaction is capped with a celebratory slide across the ice rink or a high-five. Work must be balanced with the right amount of play.

Erik chases down morning joggers, informing them of the need to refuel on their run. "You need your carbohydrates! Here, open up. I'll feed you while you run!" Erik explains, running beside two joggers. Either Erik's words are not registering, or the couple does not want a double-fudge, chocolate-chip cookie in the middle of their workout.

Brad, staying true to form and title (the world's greatest hugger), tries to bypass his language blunders by leading with a hug instead of a coffee. He also offers a special of the day: coffee and chorus. Once he has the attention of a customer he belts out: "You never close your eyes anymore when I kiss your lips. And there's no tenderness like before in your finger tips. . . ." Luckily, the gentleman is not bilingual, and a smile crosses his face.

"BUT BABY, BELIEVE ME I KNOW IT" the rest of the Crew joins in. "You've lost that loving feeling . . . now it's gone . . . gone . . . gone." Applause erupts and the coffee is hot — what more can you ask for?

After braving the morning cold, we arrive back at the hotel and take some time to answer emails. We receive requests to present at schools, plant a garden, work at a food bank. It is unlikely that we will be able to fulfill every request, but we reply to each letter sent and forward them to the Web site to be posted for others to champion. Erik casually looks at the digital pictures that will soon be uploaded. Val sits upright on his bed, his eyes closed in meditation. Brad uses his pen and poetry to express the magic of this place.

Words half grasped
slipping thru a fist like
half frozen water
on a Quebec winter shore.
Skating on thin ice, I am

here in dis world
with different sounds and new smiles
young children go where I cannot.
The radio is all French
and I find joy in the words
of a once unmusical speech
for dey first time.
I dance, understanding enough,
knowing it's a love song,
or perhaps the song of someone
who remembers another gone?
I can't quite hear the story yet
but in dis new year
I walk on water
sing in tune
taste French morning coffee.
Au revoir.

I stare out the window, light casting a warm, reflective gaze over the cold city. My thoughts drift to my brother, sitting across the hall. I think about the sacrifice Jonathon has made to be with us. A month into his last year at university, he dropped everything and dedicated himself to the tour for three months. Leaving school means not graduating; he will have to extend his studies another full year.

However, as far as Jonathon is concerned, he was already a part of the Kindness Crew. A month before the tour, Jonathon and his little brother (he was part of the Big Brothers organization) spent an afternoon on the running trails in Calgary giving out watermelon and lemonade. Later, the two involved local grocers in their kind acts and made sandwiches for the homeless. The experience was life changing for Jonathon — he was ready to take kindness on the road.

This was the longest time Jonathon and I had spent together since high school, before I went to the University of Victoria and Jonathon to the University of Calgary. Considering all of our differences in high school, it was remarkable that we had found this mutual passion. Having this mission to bring us together has filled me with a newfound purpose and passion for the project.

Within the hour the bus is packed and set to leave for yet another city. We jump aboard and steer ourselves toward the Atlantic. Taking the time to enjoy the beauty of this city has helped remind us of the importance of taking care of ourselves if we want to continue giving to others. After two months with few breaks in between, our rest has helped avoid burnout and renew our energies for the provinces ahead. We are now refuelled and ready to brave the East Coast winter.

Visit a Care Facility
or Retirement Home

1. Set up your visit.

Every community has some sort of care facility or home for seniors who require an assisted living environment, but not every community has a strong base of volunteers to visit residents regularly. Phone the administration of your local care facility and enquire about their volunteer programs, as they may already have several in place: helping serve tea one afternoon, reading to residents, or simply dropping by to play a game of chess or checkers.

2. Suggest an activity.

If you want to push the extreme kindness envelope (and we assume you do!), suggest an activity. You may want to play some music with your friends, act out a scene from a play, or run an impromptu dance! If the facility has the means, you may want to offer to help chaperone an off-site activity. A scenic tour or even cruising the local mall to do a bit of shopping may be a welcome suggestion if you have a number of keen crew members.

3. Spread the word!

Tell us your story by posting it on our Web site message board, extremekindness.com. Put the challenge out to others in your community to do the same, or team up with them and create an afternoon seniors will never forget.

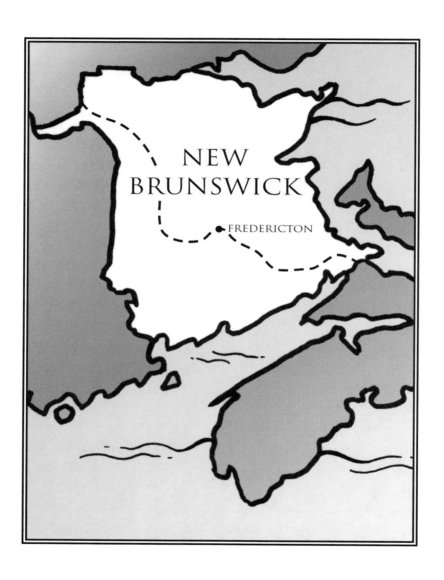

NEW
BRUNSWICK

•FREDERICTON

NEW BRUNSWICK

I have learnt silence from the talkative,
toleration from the intolerant, and kindness
from the unkind; yet strange,
I am ungrateful to these teachers.
— *Kahlil Gibran*

FREDERICTON — CHRIS

We arrive in Fredericton late at night, snowflakes flittering in the light of the street lamps. Our first night in the Maritimes will be a white one. A day early for our scheduled Kindness Marathon, we are left with two choices: find a family to take us in, or find a back road where we can park the bus for the night. Lacking in energy, we decide on the latter. Even the tiniest activity is making us tired.

We muster the strength to the put pedal to metal and the bus sweeps across the ice-coated road. With the help of a few friendly strangers we find a quaint spot to spend the night: Odell Park. Winter has left the park desolate, and we'll be free to enjoy a quiet night alone. The sub-zero temperatures force us to hurry and we erect an awning that stretches from the side of the motorhome like a swan's wing. We prepare to partake in what has become a tour ritual: the winter barbecue.

I am the weakest link tonight and therefore I must venture into the cold to cook the steaks. Standing over the hood of the barbecue, knees shivering, my senses are tortured by the mouth-watering smell of 15-ounce steaks on the grill. I think of my parents' deck and the memories of many meals that have been shared there. Even among my friends, I suddenly feel gripped by loneliness. I yearn for the familiarity and comfort of British Columbia: the mild, windswept landscape of Victoria, my room in my house, my family. Too many days have passed since I've had any contact with those at home I love.

I want to be able to share my experiences with my family, but I am at a loss to describe in just a phone call a prairie fall, winter in Old Quebec, or the taste of the Atlantic shivering my lips. How can I share with them the thousands of faces I have seen? Instead, I tell them I love them and that I appreciate the support they have given to me throughout this process, especially during the most arduous part of our journey: the year leading up to the tour when our dream seemed impossible.

Luckily, I have come to find family in those I meet during the tour. I can hear my father's laugh in the chuckle of a farmer, feel my mother in the embrace of a volunteer at a soup kitchen, and I have my brother beside me at all times. I wonder when, during my stay in Fredericton, I will find that familiar feeling of family again — whose touch will it be that reminds me that family is a small word for a big concept?

Snowed in in Fredericton.

The morning comes after one long blink and we wake to a park sugar-coated with snow. The prospect of putting fresh tracks in uncharted territory pulls us from the bus and like six year olds on a playground we dash into the great white open. Outside the motorhome a vast system of trails fans out into the park. Erik dashes down the first one and we follow, venturing deep into the forest.

Val peels the bark of a birch tree, hoping to strip a postcard-thin sheet to write home on. Erik bounces back and forth across the trail like Brad's Great Dane, searching for winter fowl. It is hard for us to imagine that a full year has passed since Brad's mother's death.

The rest of the group is stuck in a saunter, dragging

their soles through the snow, each captivated by their ability to walk on water. It is these moments in nature, whether peering over Niagara Falls, atop a prairie hill, or swimming in the summer-warmed waters of a lake in Merritt that centre us, no matter how far from home.

Our escape is short but sweet as our schedule pulls us back to the Sheraton Hotel where Dorothy, the Kindness Captain, greets us with open arms at the front door. Dorothy embraces each of us as if we were her own sons, and over the next three days we will have the privilege of experiencing her care and hospitality. She is a Maritime Mother Teresa.

Our bags are stowed (there is no time to waste!) and we are greeted by staff that seem far too happy for this early hour. Everyone sings in unison: "Hey boys! Good ta see ya! Glad ya made it this far east — saved the best far last didn't ya! Are yah ready for the big day? Ahh, this is going to be fun!" How do they muster the energy this early in the morning? The cold weather must breed this type of camaraderie and excitement. People from every area of the hotel are here: maids, janitors, servers, and managers. There will be no deterring these people from their mission.

Another gruelling gauntlet of goodwill begins by sending the mob of hotel workers onto the streets, sneaking onto trucks with croissants and hot cocoa to warm the icy fingers of construction workers, and bombarding the surrounding houses with free breakfasts and offers to shovel driveways.

Sleep-starved parents in housecoats opens doors and

surprisingly venture out into the cold, shovel in hand. Kindness, it seems, is a two-way street in this neighbourhood. This was not the response we were expecting, but things are done a little differently in these parts. In Fredericton, you always lend a helping hand — the kindness of strangers isn't just a random occurrence, it is a way of life.

The giving keeps on going — blue robes can be seen darting across the fresh snow to pass on the kindness to neighbours. Confident that kindness will continue to spread throughout the neighbourhood, a shift from suburban to urban is in order and we ready for a trip downtown.

Brad soaks up the morning sun while handing out coffee to commuters.

Val polishing up his act for the Kindness Marathon in Fredericton.

A chartered bus — better suited for a rock band than a volunteer squad — meets us and escorts us into the city's centre. We don chef hats and take trays of appetizers into the city. Party platters are decadently decorated with cream cheese smothered crackers and smoked salmon. Boxes packed with tins of black polish and bristle brushes are toted under the arms of eager shoe-shiners.

On every corner and in every doorway there is a member of the kindness crew, shining shoes or stuffing crackers in the mouths of shoppers. Dorothy and her band of merry men are bringing smiles back to the faces that have been frozen by frigid temperatures. Laughter echoes through the tiny downtown core of Fredericton and creeps in through the windows of the stores. Business is not booming yet and managers feel obliged to find out what is happening on the streets. Not ones to be left out of a good deal, shopkeepers offer items from their shelves to be distributed to pedestrians.

Everyone we encounter on the street greets us as if we are neighbours. Kindness must be a hereditary trait in the Maritimes. Has the cold climate forced people to rely on the generosity of strangers during times of strife and now kindness to strangers is the norm?

Dorothy steals us away from our downtown antics to take us on a tour of the city. "Work must be balanced with the right amount of pleasure!" she reminds us.

Crossing from one street to the next I am reminded of our colonial past, and the tour brings back a hundred history lessons nearly forgotten.

We arrive at our first stop on the tour, and Dorothy, without as much as a hint to what the location is, opens the doors to the group and says, "I've got a surprise!"

The exterior of the building gives no indication as to the business beyond its doors; there is no signage, no logo. The building more closely resembles a community centre than a cultural landmark. Dorothy pokes her head out the door and motions frantically that we are to come inside. The room looks more like a doctor's office than a store; we conclude that Dorothy has decided a checkup is in order. As much as we believe in maintaining our health, a trip to the doctor's office doesn't make our Top 10 list of preferred activities.

The receptionist directs us each to our own waiting

room where we are instructed to take off our shirts and wait. The door opens, a young practitioner walks in and asks me to lie on my stomach. I can't bear to think of the tests that will be performed. But when her hands touch my shoulders she massages my neck rather than checks my spinal alignment. I have had hairdressers massage my head, but I have never had a doctor massage out my maladies.

"Dorothy's picked up the tab for seven full massages. Surprised?"

I should have guessed. Doctors say that stress can manifest itself in a stiff neck, headaches, and lower back pain, but I could have never imagined I'd feel so rejuvenated after an hour on the table!

The next night we drag our barbecue out from the motorhome for one more cookout under winter skies. Our lack of culinary creativity and tight budget has left us with only one option: hot dogs. We are desperate to try anything new so we offer the dinner to the public — we love company. We are certain that our winter picnic will draw rave reviews; certainly no one in this town is barbecuing in these temperatures. To our surprise (unfortunately, we have not done our market research) another seller has already set up his stand and has a line-up. We send Val out to negotiate space — surely, he'll be able to convince him to welcome the competition. Surprisingly, the vendor acquiesces and business booms.

Erik is the perfect representative for recruiting given

that he is an extreme extrovert (on the streets of Toronto, Erik tried to set a Guinness Record for making eye contact and initiating conversation: 82), and he shakes the hand of every potential customer, making sure that all feel welcome. His campaigning is obviously working and a long line forms as Brad works to build a customer base, yelling to the pub-crawlers and late-night drifters, "Getttt yerrr hotdogs here!"

A man has been watching us for a half an hour, hovering 20 feet from our stand, just barely in view. He doesn't seem dressed for the temperature; his jacket is tattered and open to the cold, his baseball cap barely grazes his ears. As I approach I see that his hands are uncovered and blackened. I wonder how his fingers are able to endure it. I ask him if he will join us for a meal. He hesitates and then without a reply follows me over to the group huddling around the cooking station. His silence makes it hard to know how he feels.

Trust is hard to nurture when you live meal to meal on the streets. However, the man, Donnie, starts to open up and he tells me about the rigour of living in freezing temperatures that can kill you in your sleep or take off a finger. He talks about the reality of thievery and alcoholism.

I am curious to know how Donnie felt about me approaching him.

"When you first approached me I didn't know whether to walk away, throw a punch, or listen." He pauses and then as a gesture of trust asks, "I've seen your world, now how'd you like to see mine?"

I oblige, wanting to know more about him. Does he

have a family that loves him? Does he believe that he can still contribute to society? What has led him here? I have spoken with scores of people across the country, but have never had the chance to talk so candidly with a person living in absolute poverty.

My mother's childhood advice swirls in my head — "Christopher, do not talk to strangers!" — but I can't help but feel grateful for his offer to experience a side of life that has always been hidden from me. I decide not to travel alone — I want to capture his story on film — so Kelly and Dave join me.

We travel in the bus to a desolate manufacturing district a few minutes away. Donnie instructs us to pull up to a derelict warehouse on a wooden foundation.

"See that space between the base of the building and the ground? That's where I live. Not much, but it's where I live. It gets cold down there. The wind blows right under the building. Sometimes the police will pick me up and put me in jail for the night so I don't freeze to death."

He motions us to follow him on hands and knees. Once under the building, a whisper guides us to a corner in the darkened alcove. A candle is lit, casting a dim light over our surroundings. A few tattered couches colour the suite, cardboard boxes stick out in every direction, and mattresses line the ground. I sink into the dusty polyester cushions and wonder how many families have rested on them, how many people used them before they came to rest in Donnie's living room. It is hard not to feel like an intruder in such a foreign space.

"What is it like to live so separate from the rest of

society? You seem so isolated here. Don't you get lonely?" I ask.

"Don't mind it much. Pretty much keep to myself. Me and my cat, Timmy, get along just fine. Don't feel like being with people right now. I've been barred from the shelter because I hit a man. Had it coming to him though. He never should've hit that woman. Now, I've got to find food on my own and can't go there anymore. But people here in Fredericton are good to me. I find a way to get by."

The deep lines in his face reflect years of life spent on the streets; his alcoholism, poor diet, and the harsh conditions are aging him prematurely. I am wondering how a candle, a blanket, and some cardboard boxes keep a person warm when Donnie begins to tell his story.

"I guess, given what I've been through, I didn't have much of a chance. I started to drink to cover up the pain of my past, ended up losing my wife because of it. Not only that, but I lost my son. He lives with his mother. I get to talk to him once in a while, but I can't see him when I'm drinking. If my son ever sees this video, I just want him to know that I love him. I love him so much!"

He pauses and reaches farther into his past. "When I was a young boy my father hit me, locked me out of the house. I was left out in the snow with only a shirt on. My brother used to live here too, but he died last year, underneath the building. He'd been with me a couple years. Now it's just me and Timmy. The other night, life just seemed to hurt so much I took a lighter to myself . . . had to burn myself to make the pain go away."

He pulls up his pant leg, revealing a festering wound — a physical reminder of the mental pain that he has had to endure alone. I wondered what we could really do for this man? How could we help him change his life?

Donnie refuses any charity, telling us that he doesn't want or need anything. "I'm just glad that someone wanted to listen and that you took the time to talk. It's just nice to know that someone still cares. I still try to help, even though I live on the streets. I was once a damn good mechanic! Not too long ago, I helped a man fix his car. He tried to offer me $50. I told him I didn't want his money; I just wanted to help. It made me feel so good to know that I could."

Letting the light flicker out, we leave Donnie and thank him for allowing us into his home. Later that night his words and wisdom still whisper to me as I begin to realize that he has helped me more than I could ever help him.

MONCTON — ERIK

Instantly it seems like summer again. We run down the sand dunes at Parlee Beach outside Moncton with shirts off and pants rolled up to the knees. In the last 48 hours the temperature has climbed remarkably. The wind warms our backs as we race to be the first member of the Kindness Crew completely submerged in the Atlantic. We have made it. We have promised a coast-to-coast Canadian tour and we have delivered. Completing a tour from the Pacific to the

Hopewell Rocks near Parlee Beach.

Atlantic is something I had imagined, but the journey's actual completion is a little beyond comprehension.

The ocean splashes up to my thighs by the time I decided to commit to a dive. Instantly I am submerged. We are here. I swim as far as possible along the sandy bottom until my lungs send me to the surface. I burst out of the ocean bathed in a happiness and self-confidence I have rarely experienced. We still have almost 20 days, four Kindness Marathons, and miles to go, but I now have no doubt that we will complete the tour.

We play on the beach for about an hour, looking at shells, drawing our names in the sand, and breathing in salt air before we reluctantly pack our sandy bodies back into the motorhome and navigate to the Confederation Bridge.

Connecting with the Homeless in Your Community

1. Volunteer at your local shelter.

• To connect with the homeless or less fortunate in your community ask those running shelters and programs what might be most useful and join their band of volunteers. You can donate food, resources, or your time — all will be appreciated greatly. Bring flowers for the volunteers who tirelessly serve the less fortunate.

2. Do something on your own.

• Make bag lunches — Prepare 10 bag lunches filled with sandwiches, fresh fruit, vegetables, and drinks. Hand them out to the homeless.

• Inspire someone — Give a homeless person a piece of art or a quote that inspires you. Create your own art, or buy something that moves you.

• Ask a homeless person out for lunch (with your parent if you are under 18) — Do you have a favourite bistro for soup and sandwiches where you could take a stranger for lunch? Take the time to sit down and talk, or get it to go!

- Stop to talk — Take the time to stop and acknowledge a homeless person you may have walked by in the past. Do something kind for him and ask who else you could help.

3. Tell us about it!

Write us at thecrew@extremekindness.com. Let the world be inspired by your generosity. Think about how you want to share your story: paint a picture, write a poem, call your local newscast and challenge the rest of the community. Start a journal to record your experiences. Think about how these experiences are shaping your life.

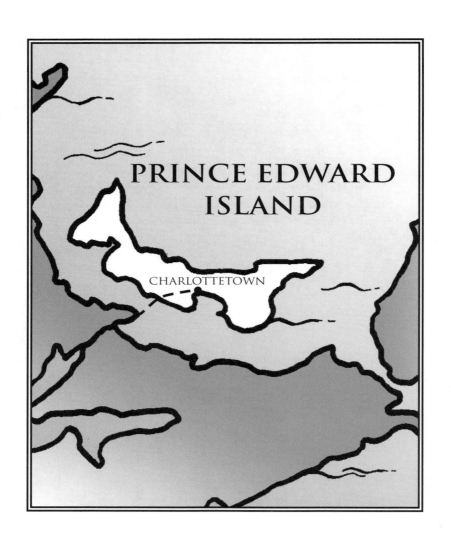

PRINCE EDWARD
ISLAND

CHARLOTTETOWN

PRINCE EDWARD ISLAND

Recompense injury with justice,
and recompense kindness with kindness.
— *Confucius*

CHARLOTTETOWN — ERIK Confederation Bridge stretches like an illumi-nated grey rainbow toward P.E.I.'s fields of red gold, the iron-rich soil treasured by farmers since colonization. Once on the island, the countryside looks like something out of a movie. Being from the west coast, I thought this scenery only existed in *Anne of Green Gables* episodes. The houses are quintessential east coast farming houses, the hills just high enough to get a view of the surrounding landscape, the towns big enough to have all the amenities but not big enough to get lost in. Charlottetown is no exception. It has no skyscrapers, no suburbs or industrial areas, and the streets are exceptionally clean.

As we roll into the Best Western we are greeted by Kevin Mouflier, the general manager, and Shelly Robinson, the Kindness Captain. After settling in we head downstairs into the smoky McLaughlin's Eatery for a staff rally. The crowd of hotel employees is not too lively initially, but they soon demonstrate a camaraderie and sense of humour. The staff is smaller than most and the rally morphs from our full presentation to a more personal discussion, during which we quickly discover that these people are no strangers to kindness. The people of Charlottetown are the kind of people who think nothing of incorporating kindness into their daily lives. For them kindness is just part of the way things work.

That evening we plan the next few days, but don't last long before we are ready for bed. After being on the road for almost two and a half months we often feel like old men who, given the choice, wouldn't stay up past 10:00 p.m. We retire to our rooms to do work but are out like a light.

"I'm sorry Erik. He just didn't make it."

The woman puts her hand on my shoulder.

"Your dad is dead. I'm really sorry."

I can't believe it. I have just spoken to my dad on the phone about my adventures, about how he has inspired me, about how, if we were the same age, he would be on this trip with us. I remember telling him how much I love him. Was that really the last time I would ever hear his voice? Would I never again feel that sense of safety?

Where am I? How did my dad die? What's happening?

It takes me a minute before I get my bearings. A wave of relief sweeps over me. I've been dreaming. It is 4:30 the morning of our Kindness Marathon in Charlottetown, P.E.I. My dad is alive and well on the other side of the country, probably just heading to bed. I take a few a deep breaths, wipe the tears from my face, write CALL DAD on my hand in black marker, and drift back into an uneasy sleep.

When I wake up to the sound of Brad singing in the shower I am still feeling upset by my dream. I sit on the bed and begin to wearily organize the day's events in my head. We don't have a press conference here, which is a bit of a relief, so the day begins with us distributing doughnuts and coffee on the street, then moves to interviews at the local radio station where Shelly's husband works, and finally to the government buildings where we offer Extreme Fitness Breaks for cramped and tired office workers. It is business as usual for the Crew but I am uncharacteristically shaken.

Brad steps out of the bathroom wearing nothing but a towel and a song and turns to me. He remarks that I look tired.

"Yeah, thanks. I had bad dreams last night."

"Did it have anything to do with your dad?"

"How did you know?"

"I know you too well, my friend."

At that moment Dave pokes his head in the door and says, "Guys, everyone is meeting in the restaurant in 10 minutes. Erik, don't forget to call your dad."

"What the . . . how did you . . . ?" Before I can get an answer he is gone. It's not until I pop into the bathroom to wash my face that I realize the wet felt from my hand has transferred itself and I have CALL DAD tattooed backwards across my cheek in big black letters.

Things quickly get out of hand and within half an hour we have a kindness roadblock in front of the hotel. Cars are backed up for a block and a half, but not one person seems to mind. In fact, these people are telling everyone they run into about it and soon half the city is eating muffins.

The morning is sunny, warm, and damp. It feels like September back home. The trees are almost bare. The enthusiastic hotel staff swarms Grafton Street carrying muffins and coffee and creating a multi-block traffic jam. We soak up some much needed sunshine. The traffic comes in waves, and during one lull a resourceful woman from the hotel decides to take a page from the extreme kindness manual and calls Charlottetown's most popular radio station, offering drive-by breakfasts to anyone who wants to come by.

"Hey thar buys. I hear yar givin' doughnuts and caaffee to any one fer free now," said one businessman too friendly to be a businessman.

"Oh, yeah!" Brad smiles, passing the man a hot coffee and a double-frosted doughnut. "We're the buys."

We are getting a kick out of the accents. We do, however, realize the necessity of practising some restraint. As soon as you start talking like you're from the East Coast you really start to enjoy it and it's pretty hard to stop. We decide that's probably how people here got started.

Hundreds of years ago someone probably began talking like that for kicks and then just couldn't shake it. Next thing you know, everyone's doing it.

Chris delivers Timbits with a smile.

After a couple of morning radio interviews we proceed to the government buildings to bring exercise into the lives of office workers.

In the lobby of the government building, Chris politely asks the receptionist, "Is the mayor in?"

I stand behind Chris dressed in a goalie mask, hockey gear, and bright red boxing pads. We have decided to go right to the top. Before the receptionist has a chance to respond the mayor pops out from behind his heavy office door, apparently en route to a meeting. He stops dead in his tracks. The surprised look on his face is justified considering we have filled the room with a dozen people carrying several forms of giant rubber exercise equipment and I look like a hybrid of Ken Dryden and Mohammad Ali.

Before he knows what is happening Chris offers me as a "human punching bag" to help him relieve some stress before his next appointment. I quickly begin to regret the offer. The mayor is not a small man and his eyes hone in on me like I am the competition in the local election. He puts his body behind a sequence of punches that suggest he might not have always been a politician. As I recover he offers the Crew city pins and asks us to sign the official town hall guestbook. He then smiles, thanks us, and hustles out the door to his meeting.

Having met the mayor we make our way through the rows of buildings to the legislative building and the next in command, Premier Patrick Binns. We sit down in the plush waiting room and Val, our most diplomatic spokesperson, approaches the slightly awestruck and stern-looking secretary.

"Hi, I'm Val Litwin and I'm travelling across the country with a group called the Extreme Kindness Crew. We would like to speak to the premier please."

"I'm afraid you don't have an appointment and he has a very busy schedule. I don't think he'll be able to see you. He's on the phone right now and he has an interview with the CBC in 10 minutes."

"That's okay, we only need a few minutes and we can wait," Chris interjects.

She looks at him, eyes narrowing. "Well, I'll let him know you're here, but I really don't think he'll have any time."

"Thanks, we'll just wait here."

The lights are dim, the music is soft, and before long we all relax. We are about to fall asleep when, true to her word, CBC shows up. The reporter and cameraman are instantly interested in what we are up to and within minutes Chris convinces them that it would be a great "day in the life" segment if they film us interacting with the premier. Premier Binns must have realized that there was no way to be interviewed without the CBC encountering us first and finally emerges from his office bearing provincial pins and a nervous smile.

All cameras are rolling as we conduct a particularly unsatisfying interview with the premier about kindness in P.E.I. To the premier's credit he does swing a few punches, but I'm not sure that he achieved a lot of stress relief. We manage to get a few nervous laughs out of him before we smother him in hugs and then leave him to the CBC interview. As we head out, he wishes us luck on the rest of the tour.

We now have the blessing of the premier and the mayor and intend to use it. We make our way into another government building and work our magic as we have in other heavily restricted buildings across the country: we smooth-talk security guards and bribe secretaries with baked good and massages. The first office is an easy sell —

we have a rather giddy secretary with a stiff neck. After five minutes she collapses like an in-box overloaded with papers.

"Actually," she confides in a hushed voice, "there are some people behind this door who could use a little stress relief. But *I* didn't tell you that."

We find people holed up in offices who look like they haven't moved since Pat Binns was elected premier in 1996. I spend more time working knots out of necks than actually receiving blows, but there is the odd office clerk who has had a rough day and is willing to go a few rounds. With giant inflatable exercise balls we storm into meetings, leaving everyone laughing.

When our energy reserves are depleted we walk back to the hotel and split up for some personal exercise time. Still trying to shake the lingering feeling of uneasiness I woke up with, I head out in the early evening with a skateboard. I'm a person who thrives on extremes and P.E.I. does not seem to be a place of extremes. I feel uninspired and out of place. I pass row upon row of perfect houses, and the shops are all the same, perfect and closed. All the shops except one, that is.

Across the street is a shop sporting a busy window full of drums and musical equipment. I listen to the exotic beats pulsing from behind the half open door and then, realizing I need to be back in time to take a shower before dinner, skate down the street. I stop suddenly and remember my dream. I decide instead to turn around to investigate. This is the kind of store my dad wouldn't pass up.

The warm smell of leather, wood, and incense fills my nostrils. The shop is devoid of people but filled with hand-carved African drums and musical instruments I have never seen before.

"Hello?"

The proprietor of the shop pokes his head out from the back room. He is wearing a hat and is dressed in loose, comfortable clothes. He is the first African Canadian I have seen in weeks.

"Hey, I'm just tightening a drum in the back. Have a look around if you like. If you need anything my name is Israel."

"What a fantastic shop. It looks like you have a lot of passion for what you do."

He looks at me, smiling, then lets out a sigh. "Thank you."

He looked like I felt. "How are you doing today?"

One simple, well-placed question was all we needed to open the gates. The conversation is deep, intimate, passionate, and heartfelt. We both feel like outsiders in P.E.I. and need to talk about the world and our places within it. We talk about the important things in our lives; for me it is my family and the tour and for him it is his family and his music. He has moved to the island to raise kids in a better environment and in doing so sacrificed his place in the vibrant musical community of Toronto. This store and the drum workshops he offers through the local schools are an outlet for his musical talents, but he really misses playing with other people of the same calibre. I think what he is doing is commendable. Just as we are wrapping up our conversation, his eyes light up and he runs to the back, returning a moment later with a homemade paper notebook and a CD in hand.

"This is the CD I just released. Look at the title!" He points at the cover: *Israel's Lost Tribes — Passionate Rhythms of Nature*. "I want you to have it. Also take this paper to write your thoughts on. I think what you are doing is wonderful."

Very rarely do I connect with someone so deeply in such a short period of time. On the skate back to the hotel I think that the shop represented exactly the kind of adventure my dad had supported and encouraged throughout my life. Perhaps my dream was a reminder to trust my heart, to open myself to the great things the world has to offer. I was beginning to realize that P.E.I. wasn't necessarily as sterile as I thought it was. The extreme is out there, you just have to be open to it.

The next morning we start the day speaking to a very receptive and polite Grade 3 class, then set off across the province to find Green Gables. Brad just happens to be a closet *Anne of Green Gables* fan but will deny it if you ask him. When we arrive, two of the friendliest park wardens I have ever met inform us that they simply don't have anything for us to do. Disappointed but not defeated, we tour the grounds then stop back at the gift shop where Brad picks up an *Anne of Green Gables* doll "for his sister."

Continuing our cross-province tour we make a bee-line for the north coast. The road follows white picket

The Crew hits the ice for a local hockey practice in Charlottetown.

fences and quaint country farmhouses. We arrive at the crashing waves, rock cliffs, and red sandy beach in the pouring rain. We play on the beach in the rain for as long as possible before heading back to Charlottetown where we have promised to assist Kevin with his son's hockey and his daughter's ringette practices.

That evening, donning gear graciously donated by a local sporting goods store, we attempt to provide some healthy competition, but not being strong skaters we make better pilons than defensemen and the kids skate circles around us.

By the time everyone is finished we are wet, cold, and

wired on the candy we have unwisely distributed to all the kids after the game. Everyone piles into the motorhome for the ride back to the hotel. Kevin's daughter cracks the window and commits what would later be dubbed "drive by shouting." A solitary man walks around a corner and looks up as she shouts, "HAVE A GOOD DAY!"

It starts to catch on. "I LOVE YOU," a boy shouts to a businesswoman walking home with groceries. The kids explode with laughter. Even the adults, who have been trying to contain themselves, are snickering.

Kevin's son has just stuffed a half a bag of M&Ms into his mouth when he spots an elderly lady walking her dog. Not being able to resist the opportunity, he jumps to the open window and lets loose something that sounds like, "AA WAAFFF OOO WIKE RAISEY!" that we think is supposed to be, "I love you like crazy."

"Did you just say 'I love you like a raisin'?"

He is laughing so hard tears are streaming down his cheeks and he has to spit out his mouthful of candy. Everyone is howling. The kids shout out that they love people like various other fruits and vegetables and by the time we have dropped everyone off my stomach is sore from laughing.

That night before bed I call home and talk to my parents. I tell them all my recent adventures, including my dream. Just hearing my dad's voice connects me with all that is great in the world and I go to bed feeling more at ease than I have for nearly three months.

Getting Political

1. Email or phone your mayor or political representative and ask her if you can have a half an hour of her time to give back to the community. Tell her you are starting a Kindness Crew and are looking for participants. Here are some suggestions for getting political:

• Venture out into the city with the mayor to shake hands and wish everyone a great day.
• Visit the police department with the mayor to thank officers for taking care of the city.
• Invite the mayor to write a letter in the local paper challenging each citizen to do one kind act.
• Make an announcement on the local television that today is Kindness Day in your community.

Write a letter to your mayor expressing your gratitude for the service she provides. Ask her to write a similar letter to the provincial premier.

2. Tell us about your experience!
Email us at thecrew@extremekindness.com. Talk to your mayor about how she felt about the experience. Include some quotes. This is the perfect way to make compassion a front-page news story. Encourage your local press to be a part of the experience.

NOVA SCOTIA

Ask yourself: Have you been kind today?
Make kindness your daily modus operandi
and change your world.
— Annie Lennox

HALIFAX — ERIK

The motorhome bumps down Highway 102 away from P.E.I. and toward our destination — Halifax, Nova Scotia. Touted as "the Victoria of the East," we eagerly await arrival in our home away from home. We have each settled into our usual positions in the motorhome. A snapshot taken at virtually any point during our travels would reveal the current scene: Brad, furrowed brow, map in lap, navigates from the passenger seat; Chris is focusing in a meditative state on the road ahead; Val listens to obscure yet soulful beats from his laptop while sprawled on the back bed; Kelly, winning his battle with bronchitis, is nestled on the couch, duvet tucked under his chin; Dave sits at the table reading a Hemingway short story; and I am relaxing in the captain's chair writing and pondering our adventures.

Not only is this port city described as one of the friendliest cities in Canada, it is also the point at which Catherine Ryan Hyde, author of *Pay It Forward*, has decided to join the tour. No one can really believe it. Though it feels like we are well acquainted, having referenced her work in virtually every media interview and press conference, we had never met Catherine. We can't wait to share our stories.

We squeeze our way through the narrow streets to the base of Citadel Hill to the appropriately named Citadel Hotel. The staff welcome us with hugs and balloons. With not a second of wasted time, Monica Smith, the hotel Kindness Captain, urges us into a limousine to the airport. Barely five minutes in town and we are already being treated like royalty. Well, truth be told, the limousine is for Catherine, but nevertheless we feel spoiled.

As the limo rolls up to the arrivals level, Chris and Val pose as "celebrities" to the people gawking on the sidewalk. They make their way into the terminal to find Catherine and return minutes later with heaps of luggage and one bona fide author.

Catherine turns out to be a natural fit with the Kindness Crew. A witty conversationalist with a dry sense of humour, she is a woman who is focused on positive goals and knows how to reach them. During the ride back into the city we talk like old friends catching up. Our discussion covers everything from the movie inspired by her book, to the publishing industry, to kindness in the United States and the prospect of an American Extreme Kindness tour. No other group that she is aware of is applying her theory on such a grand a scale.

Little do we know that the relationship cemented on this visit will encourage Catherine to assist a financially destitute Kindness Crew by purchasing our Web site, www.extremekindness.com, from an Internet pirate who has purchased our expired domain name. Aside from being a strong supporter and an experienced sounding board, Catherine becomes a good friend. We hope that by continuing the project our appreciation for all that she has done is self-evident.

Free, fresh-baked cookies. What's the catch?

The next day we plan to put Catherine's words into action after our first East Coast press conference and several interviews at the local radio station. We are distributing sweaters, scarves, fresh-baked muffins, warm cookies, and hot coffee on Spring Garden Avenue. When the time comes, everyone sports tall chefs' hats and white Kindness Crew T-shirts and floods the streets. The group is large and enthusiastic and apt to embrace spontaneous acts of kindness. Hotel associates are sprinting into office buildings and giving massages. Cars are stopped mid-street, their drivers offered breakfast. Sweaters are passed to anyone looking like they might be even slightly chilled.

"This is seriously fun," one housekeeper shrieks as she helps a tourist with directions and offers her a hug. "He didn't know what to think. All I did was tell him where a restaurant was and give him a hug. He just kept smiling and saying thank you."

The four of us manage to stay together as a team, but Catherine is quickly kidnapped by a group of enthusiastic hotel managers on a mission to find homeless people in need of clothes.

Val strikes up a conversation with a boisterous, but down on his luck, street poet about the collection he is selling. Brad, taking Val's conversation as a cue, snatches a copy of the poet's collection and begins serenading young women with verses from its pages. Chris, salesman extraordinaire, offers it to pedestrians at a price of $2, a limited time offer (the original price being $1).

Copies of the poet's work are going like hotcakes so, realizing my services can be better used elsewhere, I offer to help a petite woman carrying a large office chair to a career search seminar. When we get there, she invites me in to speak. I join the class for an impromptu presentation on the Extreme Kindness Tour. When I return to the poetry corner Chris and Brad are interviewing a couple of teenage girls who offer a testimonial.

"We were having the worst day, seriously, but you guys made it so much better. This is the first good thing that has happened to us all day. Thank you so much. What you guys are doing is fantastic. We will definitely pay this forward."

A downtown sporting goods store called Cleves hosts lunch and is the delivery drop for a shipment of giveaways from Columbia Sportswear. As we sit on the sidewalk eating our lunch the store manager informs us that the shipment has been delayed and will not arrive until next week. Seeing the despondent looks on our faces he searches amid the store's stock for Columbia gear we can use instead. A half-hour later he emerges grinning with a box full of gloves, toques, and headbands. We assemble the remaining hotel employees and Catherine and set about warming up the city one head and hand at a time. And then we get an idea.

Armed with a box of essential oils for aromatherapy, nail polish, chocolate-covered strawberries, cucumber slices, a giant green stability ball, yoga mats, blankets, and a couch from the hotel (that "probably wouldn't be noticed" if it went missing for a few hours), we march downtown wearing nothing but white terry towel robes. People stop their cars. Passersby burst out laughing. By the time we reach our destination Kelly has enough footage to cut together something for *America's Funniest Home Videos*. We set up our Extreme Spa Experience in the middle of the sidewalk on one of the busiest corners in Halifax, the corner of Spring Garden and South Park. Within 10 minutes, massage chains have formed and people are talking about the benefits of kindness.

Brad is sitting on the sidewalk in front of the couch giving pedicures, foot massages, and painting toenails. He has towels wrapped around his legs, sports a frog toque, and wears pink children's sunglasses. As more people join the crowd of onlookers the media gathers. We have a live feed with CBC Newsworld, but also have two local papers, two local radio stations and a Web 'zine. The CBC crew are there as part of a live forum on volunteerism in Canada, so every 20 minutes we pile on to the couch to talk about our adventures in altruism to be broadcast to the entire country.

Often genuine kindness is thought of as antiquated, inefficient, not the stuff of "real" news. By simply hauling a couch onto the street in December and lightheartedly offering a massage we are changing public perception. Our tour is a prime example of how to create something that's simple, fun, and worthy. Through this kind of media coverage kindness becomes current.

After spending several hours in sub-zero temperatures with minimal clothing, it starts to snow and we decide to shift our activities to a warmer venue. Taking advantage of the large crowds we follow Catherine into a friendly cell phone store where we drink gallons of hot chocolate and she signs copies of *Pay It Forward* for several excited fans. Late that afternoon we hike back through the snow, cursing the heavy couch.

The Festival of Lights is on that evening, and I hatch a last-minute plan to try to sneak the motorhome into the parade as part of the festivities, decked out in Christmas lights, of course. We scrounge together lights from the Citadel Hotel's supply and attempt to drape them from the Kindness Cruiser. Brad, Val, and Jonathon look like the three stooges trying to rig the electrical system for power while Chris and I attempt to attach the lights. We have just found the perfect balance of grace and duct tape when the electrical engineers give up and make it clear that my latest crazy scheme will not see the light of day. Grudgingly, we leave the vehicle in the hotel parking lot and, dressed in red Columbia jackets, saunter off in the direction of the festivities.

The parade is spectacular. There are people walking or rolling down the street dressed up as everything from Santa Claus to Farmer Bill. Lacking a float of our own, we join someone else's for the duration. The polka float seems the most logical choice — the music is good, the float is beautiful (not to mention the dancers, OmmPaPa!), and we get to dance. Perhaps it's the season, perhaps it's the media coverage we'd received, perhaps it's the hugs, but before long several people have joined the Kindness Crew and are recruiting others by jumping on and off the float.

After hugging, dancing, and laughing, we leave the parade for a potluck and then an evening out to take full advantage of the Halifax nightlife.

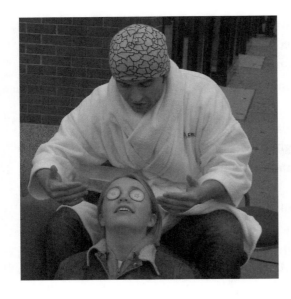

Val applies icy cucumbers to eyes of a weary Haligonian during the Ultimate Spa Experience in Halifax.

The next morning we join Catherine to discuss the possibility of writing a book. Her calm, composed, and professional approach makes us feel that whatever we are about to discuss is of great importance. She is very supportive of the idea and offers suggestions about how to make it happen, even offering to write the foreword.

For the first time in months we are within an hour of surfable ocean and after breakfast I leave on a mission. The beaches north of Halifax host some of the most beautiful point and reef breaks in Canada. Being an avid surfer and surf instructor from the West Coast I am determined to snag a few waves and to teach a novice how to do it with me. I discover the Dacane Surf Shop tucked away on the corner of Blower and Grafton Streets and meet its owner, Lance Moore.

Lance opened the shop a couple of years ago and is at the epicentre of surfing on the East Coast. He does everything he can to support the local scene, including sponsoring contests each year. I explain the tour to him and that I plan to teach someone while here. I leave with three boards, three neoprene wetsuits, and directions to the beach.

The beach at Laurencetown sends chills down my spine. Not only is it one of the most beautiful places I have seen in Canada, the air temperature registers just above zero. I enter the ocean as the strong offshore wind whips hail into my face. Each time I duckdive an icy wave my face tightens, and I feel like I have just eaten an ice cream cone too fast. After stroking into a few small glassy waves which peel nicely across the bay, I decide the beach is safe and I paddle in to grab my two enthusiastic surf students, Maggie and Linda Cummins. Perhaps enthusiastic is too strong a word, but I am certain I hear squeals of excitement as the freezing rain whips their wetsuits.

We had met Maggie the previous day during the Kindness Marathon and had stuck up a conversation about surfing. She said she had always wanted to learn and immediately the boys offered my services as an instructor. I'm not sure she thought we would go through with it, but this morning when we knocked on her door she was ready and her sister was keen to join, too. She has no idea what she is getting into.

It isn't warm, but at least it isn't flat. The wind has

picked up considerably and it is virtually impossible for the girls to carry the nine-foot beginner boards down the beach. After explaining tides, currents, and ocean safety, I opt to start with a body surfing lesson and we go sprinting down the beach into the waves. The increase in icy wind makes the water feel like fire. After 30 seconds our faces, our only exposed skin, are completely numb. Maggie and Linda wade out together, bob in the water, and start swimming toward shore at the sight of a big wave on the horizon. The wave swells underneath us and suddenly we are surfing. The sensation of weightlessness, water rushing on all sides, is truly magical. Before we know it the ocean has gently deposited us up the beach on the soft sand. The girls have perma-grins on their faces and are sprinting back down the beach for more. We stay out until hypothermia begins to set in then run

The dark and stormy waters near Laurencetown.

back to the warmth of the vehicle.

With hail pelting our skulls and wind blowing the boards in every direction, the girls get changed and Jonathon and I tie the boards back to the roof, jump back in the motorhome, and head back to the city. Mission accomplished!

The next day we say a tearful goodbye to Catherine. By the time each of us has given her a hug and Kelly has wrapped up his last interview, we deputize her a member of the Kindness Crew. At the press conference the previous day she had said, "As you can see (holding up her Kindness Crew T-shirt) I *am* the Kindness Crew," so we decided to make it official.

With promises of future adventures together she is whisked off to the plane bound for home.

We fill the rest of the morning with meetings at the hotel, cleaning, editing, and packing the motorhome for Newfoundland. I manage to avoid most of the work and sneak out for another surfing adventure with Lance. I hadn't planned to surf again, but in the words of the immortal Lance Moore, "How can you pass up a perfect East Coast swell? They don't come very often and really, when are you going to be in Halifax again?"

I return later that afternoon after surfing perfectly peeling overhead waves. I am now truly a Canadian surfer. That night as we roll through a blizzard toward the ferry terminal at North Sydney I reflect on how lucky we are to be warm, safe, and bound for an island adventure. If

Newfoundland lived up to its reputation as Canada's kindest and most eccentric province, we would fit right in.

Extreme Acts of Kindness

1. If someone on your Crew is into surfing, skateboarding, rock climbing, skydiving, horseback riding, mountain climbing . . . and is comfortable sharing her skills with others wisely and safely, encourage her to do so.

2. Help others overcome their fears, increase their self-esteem, and perhaps even have a life-changing experience.

**3. Email your story to
thecrew@extremekindness .com**
What is your extreme skill? How did you feel about sharing it with someone else? How did your protegé react?

NEWFOUNDLAND

I have always depended on the
kindness of strangers.
— Tennessee Williams

PORT AUX BASQUES — VAL

At the eastern edge of continental Canada where land meets infinite liquid, where to travel farther requires wings, wood, or wit — often all three — there resides a rock, or rather, The Rock. As much as people complain about land masses that aren't attached to mainlands by the modern umbilical cords of architecture and engineering, no one will deny that there is still something soul-stirring about a ferry ride. I've lived on an island my whole life and always considered the extra effort required to get home a kind of affirmation, a gesture of my love for the isolation that only a true islander can know. I began this journey with a ferry passage and now I am ending it with one.

A fierce gale has begun to blow; winter has swiftly veiled the land in snow. The motorhome rocks violently as we hurtle down the Trans-Canada. The wind unravels and rips our canopy off the side of the camper. Erik, Brad, and me, venture out into the frigid winds to mount the icy roof and repair the damage with plastic grocery bags. The cold is so vicious we come back into the motorhome with splitting headaches. Our generator is fickle at best and on nights with no heat we have to bunk down in ski pants, layers of fleece, and three to a bed just to keep warm.

After a five-hour wait and news that the five-hour passage "could take up to 16, depending on the weather," we join the hitchhikers, semi-drivers, and hobos sleeping in the chairs. We have been travelling for over 90 days; arriving on the shores of Newfoundland signals the end of our journey. Gander and St. John's, here we come. November 28th will be the final day of the tour.

Our journey aboard the MV *Caribou* from North Sydney to Port aux Basques is 96 nautical miles. Our Northern Baltic 1A Super houses a crew of 68. She shudders and thumps her way across the strait, sending plumes of spray and walls of water off the beam strong enough to disrupt the swell. Apart from the odd visit to the outer deck, our time is spent on the vacant sofas, heads and legs dangling off either end, drooling in pseudo-sleep. Our evening meals, harvested from several of the ship's sundry vending machines, will quickly fade from memory. A Five Alive aperitif and a modest entrée of Doritos chips is the healthiest combination my $2.50 can muster.

Val aboard the ferry heading to Port aux Basques.

The first glimpse of Newfoundland couldn't be more impressive. Tucked tightly into a wind shadow on the upper deck with my back up against the ship's cold steel, nylon hood slapping my face, Newfoundland appears through tears brought on by the cold. I can make out rocky bluffs dusted by ice and purpled by the dying light of day, then — like being surprised by a familiar face — I look off the starboard bow and find a perfectly round moon lifting out of the rock, glowing a borrowed orange.

For a moment I am immobilized by the sheer spectacle of it rising out of the cold, grey landscape; it's literally breathtaking. It's the kind of moon you want to remember forever so you stare and stare in the hopes that it will burn its circular brightness into your memory. I shut

An aerial view of The Rock.

my lids a few times to see it in the dark, just to make sure it's still there, a residual image floating in a sea of black. I rush below deck to grab the others. After spending so many days with the guys, every experience has to be shared to be appreciated. The moon won't look as bright unless Chris, Brad, and Erik see it too.

Once the ship docks we make a break for Cornerbrook. It's a bleak drive. There are very few streetlights and winds pummel the vehicle. A mild ice storm has thickened the air and ice crystals are flying in all directions. We make it to Cornerbrook in six hours and spend the night in a mall parking lot.

There is no running water since the motorhome pipes have been emptied to avoid frozen, ruptured plumbing. Unfortunately, there are no supermarkets on the horizon this morning and it looks like a snowdrift will have to suffice for the water supply. We scoop handfuls of snow to munch on and wet our toothbrushes. Apart from last night's pizzeria, the snowdrift is about all we'll see of the town.

Gander doesn't expect us for several days so we have scheduled a day and a night of rest and reflection at Gross Morne National Park. There have still been no moose sightings and Gross Morne, every Newfoundlander has boasted, is the Promised Land.

It is a peaceful moose-on-the-mind kind of day when Jonathon shouts, "Woman in need! Woman in need!" Chris is at the helm and immediately slows and pulls off to the side of the road. We come to a rough halt like a ship running aground. All the Crew can see, save Jonathon, is frozen land, shimmering in the sun. Sadly lacking is a damsel; also absent is her partner, distress.

We have travelled almost the entire breadth of Canada and are beginning to wonder if we are ever going to shovel snow. Every time a reporter questioned, "What sort of acts of kindness are planned for the tour?" our perennial answer was, "Shovel driveways!" It was the perfect image of kindness, a simple act that said so much, but required so little and, really, what could be more Canadian than hefting snow? Forget the CBC, forget maple syrup, even forget the holy sport of hockey, it is this noble winter pastime that unites us all. If it were an Olympic sport, Canada would control the field — total domination, no competition, no mercy. If the Inuit have 100 names for it then every Canadian has 100 ways of scooping, shoving, salting, blowing, plowing, melting, moving, quarrying, excavating, and digging it.

We have found our calling: a middle-aged woman struggling to clear her driveway and free her Ford Bronco. There are not enough shovels or snow to slake our thirst for it. We don't just shovel it, we sculpt it, cradle, and relocate it. Audrey, the damsel, watches us in distress, swimming in a grey duffel coat too large for her frame, her shiny blue gumboots planted.

We are feeling Canadian to the core and the job is almost done, but something curious is happening as we work. During the shovelling several neighbours have wandered from their homes and are crunching up the street right into Audrey's house. Even more curious: each carries a massive piece of Tupperware. Though Audrey has not talked to anyone since we arrived, the news seems to have travelled.

Inside, crocheted tea cozies, popsicle-stick reindeer, homemade walnut wreaths, colourful knitted blankets, a wooden map of Newfoundland bedecked with a collection of silver tea spoons, and four mystery guests pack her kitchen. Lining the plate rail is a collection to rival any, including the most appropriate, which reads: "A man's greatness can always be measured by his willingness to be kind."

"That's one of my favourites," says Audrey.

On the table moist molasses biscuits, soft muffins, gooey date squares, lemon bars, chocolate-zucchini brownies, oatmeal-raisin cookies, cheese scones, and four pots of tea have been prepared by Audrey's three sisters. Our first Newfoundland encounter is becoming more and more magical by the minute.

"We all grew up on this very street. We've never been more than 30 paces from each other our whole lives."

"And when guests show up we go to our pantries, fill our Tupperware, and march right up to the party!" The sisters are hilarious, finishing each other's sentences and mothering us like their own.

Another 28 hugs are traded in the crowded kitchen and we thank the sisters heartily for sharing their family recipes with us. The sound of zippers and swish of ski pants signal our exit and we crunch off down the road, tummies full and hearts warm.

GROS MORNE — VAL

Soon we will be atop a misty summit looking down a glacier-carved fjord thousands of feet deep. The Newfoundland Tourism Web site describes it this way:

> *Ramble over an ancient expanse of mantle rock where colossal collisions of tectonic plates created formations as barren as the moon. Take a stroll through a jumbled mass of rust-colored rocks. Visit the Tablelands, a 600-metre high plateau that forms one of the world's best examples of rock exposed from the earth's interior, rock usually found only deep beneath the ocean floor. This is the land of the Titans, where human travellers are dwarfed by Precambrian cliffs towering thousands of feet above land-locked fjords.*

The land of Titans, indeed. In addition to bakeapple berries and the 30 wild species of orchid, we are on the lookout for an elusive woodland moose. To say we have become obsessed with this even-toed herbivore would be an understatement: this droopy-lipped, humped creature has become the Holy Grail, the very spirit of Canada and kindness. The moose is a much more appropriate national mascot than the beaver. For starters, its sheer size is more representative of our sprawling country than the European compactness of the beaver. The moose's giant hump is a faithful ode to the many mountain ranges that typify our bumpy expanse, and as a species it can be found in all corners of the world just as the Canadian populace is global in its origins. Moose can be found munching moss from Wyoming to Siberia, or flapping their nasal apertures from the banks of the Yenisey to the plains of Manchuria. It's rarely assertive and typically keeps to itself, trotting off contentedly at the first whiff of conflict. Its unusual appearance, lumbering gait, and giant flap of skin are something to laugh at, and we Canadians love to laugh.

Outfitted with enough digital cameras to document any moose sighting, we wander the cold tundra of Newfoundland's most famous park. It is a bitterly cold hike, but there is no wind and we wander in complete silence. Snow hangs from hard and scrubby-looking trees, giant bonsais gone to seed. Our path is taking us over the Tablelands to a lake and beside that lake is . . . a moose. It is the most anticlimactic and exhilarating moment of the trip.

"I don't see anything," Brad says.

"Me neither," agrees Dave.

"Yup, nothing." My eyes are straining.

"Kelly, would you do us a favour and call it again?"

Jonathon refers to Kelly's yelp that passes for a mating call.

Because none of us have binoculars we are forced to use the zoom function on our cameras, hoping desperately that we can capture something on film. We feel like we're looking for the Sasquatch. We can't make out a distinct shape, just a large furry mass hidden in a fuzzy mess of trees and scrub. We resemble a group of horribly amateurish filmmakers shooting the world's most pathetic nature documentary. We are wearing the brightest red winter garb imaginable and are yelling like we are on the floor of the Toronto Stock Exchange. There is no way our film is going to make it to the Outdoor Life Network.

Then it moves.

There it is, standing with its big furry butt to us, dipping its head every now and again to chomp lichen or whatever moss-de-jour it has found beneath the snow. It is in a thicket of young pines. Was this moment ridiculous or reverent?

"His giant butt is facing us!" Jonathon laughs, answering my question. The eight-foot-tall creature is mooning us. We have travelled almost 100 days for this moment; it was pregnant with significance and this is what we get.

Just then Gros Morne's finest spots the ragtag paparazzi across the lake. The collective reek of seven men who haven't showered in four days finally wafts over the water and the animal as-seen-in-its-natural-habitat makes a break for fresher smelling pastures.

Chris tries to console us. "We shouldn't rule out the likelihood of hitting one on the way to St. John's; there

Beware moose crossing in Gros Morne.

have been 40 moose-related accidents in the past 10 months alone — some fatal." Chris pats my back. It was true, signs peppered the highway warning of mating moose who mistake small Ford Festivas for objects of desire.

If the moose really is the spirit of Canada and kindness then, even though it is often hidden, it's still all around us. Newfoundlanders and guidebooks both likened the ubiquitous Newfoundland moose to fish off the Grand Banks — there are thousands of them, but just below the surface. Hiding, but alive and well, striding vigorously through the underbrush of Canadian soup kitchens, subways, coffee shops, bus stops, movie theatres, gas stations, supermarkets, schools, and homes. It seems even more appropriate that our eventual encounter with that lovely creature was a funny one. People often asked us on the road why we placed so much emphasis on making kindness fun. "Isn't kindness enough all by itself? Why make it fun?" But there you have the answer: when one person laughs others join in.

GANDER — VAL

Typically, arrival in a new town signalled high phone bills because we had to call the hotel's front desk for directions. This time the general manager phoned *us* from the hotel and told us to meet her at the gas station up the road. Newfoundlanders are passionate people, whether they're listening to Celtic music in pubs packed fuller than seine nets or pulling travellers off the street for a warm meal and a place to sleep. We were about to find out just how passionate.

When we pulled in, Jonathon opened the door and a small fist gripping pink carnations thrust through the opening. Peggy was accompanied by Gander's Chief of Police Holmes, our escort.

Gander prides itself on its giving spirit. During the September 11th crisis the residents of Gander hosted scores of flights that had been grounded. The town's population of 6,000 doubled in a matter of hours.

Families opened their homes to complete strangers and there wasn't a couch in town that didn't have somebody sleeping on it. Web sites have sprung up all over the Internet devoted to the stories and pictures of Americans who had their hearts stolen by Gander's inhabitants. A huge party was thrown in New York to honour the Newfoundland families who took in those frightened travellers. Better the spirit of giving define a town than a giant hockey stick or a gargantuan plaster hot dog.

Chief Holmes wove through every residential side street, rolled by every strip mall, and cruised every school. His lights were whirling full blast, like a blender set to purée. Ladies in lime-green puffy parkas, fresh from the supermarket, held rattan shopping bags at the elbow and stopped to wave as we passed. Kids ran up to their chain-link fences in schoolyards. After a 20-minute tour-de-Gander we are greeted by hotel staff singing Newfoundland's unofficial folk anthem: "You Gotta Be Happy."

This morning we hit the suburbs, wearing Santa hats and clip-on reindeer antlers, with cookies and enough canisters of hot cocoa to fill an Olympic-sized hot tub. Employees with trucks fill their flatbeds with goodies and cocoa until they look like portable pantries. The kindness motorcade (four cars and one 34-foot motor-home) belts Christmas carols from its open windows. It is quite a sight to see full grown men and women hurdling small hedges, double-fisting hot chocolate, cookies in plastic wrap clenched between teeth, and running up to front doors only to ring doorbells with their noses.

In his movie *Bowling for Columbine,* Michael Moore is amazed to discover how relaxed most Canadian's are about home security, most — Moore concludes — are more worried about trapping themselves *in* their homes with their high-tech alarms than they are about keeping others *out.*

I leap one hedge, slopping a minimal amount of cargo, and a man watching from his living room gives me a look that says, "Nice hurdle, good height, and solid landing!" He shows up at his front door beaming, "I'll take two cookies: got any oatmeal raisin?" Paranoid, Newfoundlanders are not.

A moment of rest on eastern shores as the coast-to-coast tour concludes.

ST. JOHN'S — VAL As the motorhome rolls down Water Street, North America's oldest commercial street, we have our first real glimpse of St. John's. The history and significance of the place are impressive. Just a short drive away, at Cape Spear, we can rightly say we stand closer to a pint of Guinness in Ireland than a hockey stick in Thunder Bay. From the top of Cabot Tower on Signal Hill, at the mouth to the harbour, Guglielmo Marconi waited faithfully for the first transatlantic wireless signal on December 12th, 1901. Old World buildings and houses painted vibrant reds, blues, and greens drift past our windows as the fabled cobblestones of George Street shake the motorhome.

The water in the harbour is a glassy dark green; above, seagulls etch playful patterns in the air. Just beyond the protection of the surrounding granite lies a windswept seascape that has, for over 500 years, swallowed hundreds of vessels and hosted numerous battles. But, sitting on the docks looking up at the granite arms that surround the harbour, I feel comforted, like I am being embraced.

The Crew is mellow and exultant as we drive through the narrow streets, windows rolled down, breathing in the salt air. The motorhome has reached the place where it will make its proverbial U-turn — this is the end of the road. Almost 100 days from Vancouver and just now touching the other side. Though the Trans-Canada couldn't pave itself farther if it tried, and we are as far away from home in our own country as we can possibly be, this still feels like home. You can see it in our relaxed faces. Perhaps it's just being in a coastal town again after three months.

A fog hangs in the air, and reports say a winter storm is racing toward the city bringing heavy snowfall. The next day we have to make a 16-hour break for the ferry in Port aux Basques.

*Swabbing the decks of the
Funk Island Banker.*

But how could we visit a port town that has been a fishery since the 15th century and not do something for the fishermen? Brad, the tour dramatist, has visions of heroically gutting giant salmon, filleting tuna, or scrubbing the deck of *every* ship in the harbour. We settle on one, *The Funk Island Banker*, we think needs a bit of grunt work.

"Forget the mops. We'd have to zamboni those decks."

"I'm boarding her!" Erik says, chomping a pencil between his teeth and grimacing, "Permission to come aboard," as he sprints up the gangplank.

The captain greets us in his galley, enjoying a lunch of "tohr-but," and informs us that he needs several tons of flat cardboard boxes on the wharf moved into the holding tank. "Mind the men outside don't slip into the wahhter when passing the cargo."

Our team workhorse loves the sound of the task set before us. Erik — the man who agreed to harvest a field of alfalfa in Saskatchewan only if he could do the whole thing — is in his element. Erik's energy is kinetic and, as always, infectious. We all de-layer, tossing fleeces and winter jackets to the side, stripping down to tank tops and T-shirts. Erik, Brad, Chris, and I stand there in a pile of clothes, staring at our support crew.

Chris pipes up, "This ain't a four man job." Jonathon rolls up his sleeves immediately while Dave and Kelly pretend to look like they've been punched in the stomach.

"I've gotta film, right?" Kelly jokes. Kelly knows he has been conscripted and there will be no draft dodging today. He turns off the camera and sets it down.

"C'mon Dave, this is a *real life* experience," Chris hustles, "you can write about it later . . ." Dave liked to pretend it was better he maintain a professional distance "for the sake of the story," but he jumped right in and we became seven strong.

Chris climbs outside and starts tossing boxes off a truck loaded so high its tires are bulging. Kelly catches them and hands them to Dave who stands on the edge of the slippery wharf. Stacks of boxes are hefted along the line, down the ladder, and into the holding tank. It feels like we are stoking a massive furnace with enough fuel to burn for a thousand years.

The muscles are moving now and sweat is soaking our shirts. Everyone is laughing and Brad begins to lead us through an amusing work song. Except we aren't working; we're having the time of our lives.

Kindness in Your Neighbourhood

1. Neighbour niceties.

Visit a neighbour who needs a helping hand, or someone 10 houses down who you've never met before, and do something for them. Here are some ideas:

- Bake a cake.
- Show up with cleaning equipment to scrub the kitchen.
- Fill mailboxes with compliments scribbled on scraps of paper.
- Wash your neighbour's car or windows.
- Wheel your barbecue next door and grill up a few hot dogs.
- Babysit.
- Mow the lawn.
- Leave them flowers.
- Put a sign in their front lawn that reads "World's Greatest Neighbour!" (you get the picture).

2. Spread the word!

Tell us your story by posting it on our Web site message board, www.extremekindness.com. Put the challenge out to others in your community to do the same or team up with them and create a day of neighbourhood kindness.

LOOKING BACK

'BRAD'

Finishing our Canadian tour was anticlimactic; the irony was that as a group of friends we were just *beginning* our adventures in kindness. I was a different person than I was before this long jaunt across my country. The tour and all that had followed had made me into a professional public speaker, motivating corporate staff, school children, and individuals. In particular I was impressed with the corporations we worked with and the positive effect they had on their communities. Allowing employees to put their hearts into their work in more ways than one is a refreshing change in a world too often motivated by financial gain. Working with all of these individuals was as challenging and as rewarding and enjoyable as writing about it. Personally, these experiences allowed me to move beyond the grief of losing my mother so that helping others helped me in return. I no longer felt dragged down by painful memories and sad farewells. My mother's death drove all of us to accomplish great things and to look for answers to hard questions: How do you live life to its fullest? Where do we go next? Perhaps the answers are interrelated. I hope we will expand the tour to bring kindness to those in other countries as well — even if it takes us the rest of our lives. I believe this book is only the first step to realizing that dream. One day I hope to claim kindness not just as my passion, but as my lifelong career.

As we drove home across a frosted Canada we allowed body, mind, and spirit to recuperate: sleeping, watching DVDS on laptops, mellowing to Sting or recordings of Stuart McLean. But all of us wrote. Everyone was still grappling with the immensity of what had taken place. Faces stared thoughtfully at computer screens as fingers hovered over the keys, tapped, paused, then tapped some more. We needed to commit to memory all those funny anecdotes, tearful moments, epiphanies, and resolutions. Life suddenly stretched out before us like the twinkling Trans-Canada. Anything was possible.

When I decided to scribble out a few resolutions for the new year fast approaching, I was surprised by what surfaced: "Give more of yourself and spend more time with your friends." I had done *nothing but* give of myself and spend time with some of the people I loved most for three months and yet nothing seemed more pressing than to welcome the new year with more of the same.

For those lucky enough, or perhaps for those who just listen carefully, the universe whispers its wisdom. This journey had been the greatest gift and it had yielded a voice that whispered, "This is just the beginning." Sitting at the back of the motorhome, feeling the bumps and contours of the road somewhere in the white country-side of Quebec, I realized a huge part of my future had already been scripted. The words of a young boy from White City, Saskatchewan, echoed in my head as we returned home: "If you want to have fun for an hour watch television, if you want to have fun for a day go to an amusement park, if you want to have fun for a life-time — help others."

The Extreme Kindness Tour was easily the greatest road-trip of my life! Our kind acts took us off the beaten track — to soup kitchens, shelters, offices of city mayors, and onto the backs of rusted red tractors. By including altruism in our adventures, I was able to connect with people who saw me not as a tourist, but as someone willing to give back to a community that was not his own. I was able to change the lives of people I had met only for a moment, and leave a karmic footprint that can never be erased.

While travelling across Canada, I also embarked on an inner journey. By practising compassion and kindness, I was able to confront and conquer a fear that had gripped me for most of my life. Although it was largely unrecognized by those around me, I have had a phobia of speaking in public for most of my life. The tour forced me to speak in front of audiences, giving me the chance to make perfect through practise. However, it was not just the sheer volume of speaking engagements that brought me new-found comfort, but what I was speaking *about*. Having something I believed in so passionately gave me the purpose that made the difference — it gave me the motivation and energy I needed to overcome my debilitating fear. Also, in learning to love others more, I learned to accept myself and feel at peace. By taking the focus off myself and placing it on the welfare of those around me, I was able to slow the anxious, inner struggle that had plagued me for so long.

Keeping to our credo of "Kindness 24/7" was, at times, a challenging endeavour. Imagine having to smile for 109 days! However, when I found myself about to react negatively to a situation or a person, I would remind myself of my mission: to connect the world through kindness. As with meditation, I returned my mind to the mantra that would help me focus. I didn't always act the way I wanted, but I realized the number of times I faltered was less important than the frequency with which I returned to compassion. Kindness, I have realized, is something that needs to be cultivated, like any new skill. Because of my commitment to compassion, I found myself able to give of myself in a way that I never would have thought possible.

If there is one thing that I hope people realize after reading about our adventures in altruism, it's that there is infinite power in extending our hands and our hearts to others. I think I have finally realized the truth of the statement, "It is in the giving that we truly receive."

"Listen to your heart" — it's a cliché that has been interpreted a thousand different ways. I suppose it's a truism that is passed on from teachers, parents, and friends to guide you in any situation. When I was leaving home for the first time, my dad passed me a wallet-sized square of paper with the quote from Act 1 Scene III of *Hamlet*, Polonius' parting words to his son Laertes. It's a list of fatherly advice on how to live a good life and ends with the famous, "This above all: to thine own self be true, / And it must follow, as the night the day, / Thou canst not be false to any man."

I have carried this with me for years, literally and figuratively, and it has helped me through difficult times.
To thine own self be true — what did it mean within the
context of my own life? The tour was an exploration of
my true self, of my heart; it was an education.

The tour created opportunities for me to focus my passion, to speak before crowds of people, to be organized
and concise as well as genuine. These skills were refined in
business meetings, media interviews, and public speaking
engagements, and provided me with an opportunity to
connect with people and make a difference.

The tour also reinforced how much you can get done
when great friendships propel you toward great things.
Their support grounded me; their love and genuine
acceptance taught me how to push my mind to see problems not as barriers, but merely as obstacles, to diligently
persist to find a solution. They taught me how to find a
positive place within myself, drawing on the friendships
around me. They have inspired me to express myself in
a way that is unique and beautiful. These friends participated in a journey that changed my life. They helped
me to listen to my heart, to tap into inspiring moments
to find the motivation for what I really wanted to do.
I found a balance between head and heart that made
things happen in my life, and in the lives of others. I
learned to be true.

Chris and Brad wave goodbye to this window of opportunity . . .

CONCLUSION

The headline of the August 28th, 2002, article in the *Globe and Mail* announcing our tour was phrased as a question: "Will Canada Embrace Kindness of Strangers?" Just under a year later, on July 23rd, 2003, the *National Post* ran an article titled, "Kindness Begins at Work." The image accompanying this story was a picture of us dressed in costumes entertaining kids on city streets, a picture from the tour. So deeply rooted in Canadian consciousness was our Kindness Marathon that even a year later major newspapers were still

Val and Erik back *in action*

telling our story. From prairie hay-towns to the breezy fishing ports of the Atlantic provinces, Canadians *craved* kindness, and according to laws of supply and demand they also provided it.

During the tour and in the months since, we have done our best to lay the foundations for an endless Kindness Marathon. That legacy of generosity would be the greatest tribute. What was once a crew of four friends is now a Kindness Crew of thousands, stretching the breadth of Canada. These satellite Kindness Crews can now be found everywhere: in schools, businesses, apartment buildings, hotels, playgrounds, subways, day camps — the list goes on.

In the year and a half that has passed since our journey, much of our time has been spent speaking at schools, showing students footage from the road, and sharing our stories. We still believe the key to a kinder world is getting the next generation hooked on giving. It has not been difficult. Youth are more conscientious and self-aware than they are given credit for, and are continually impressing us with their enthusiasm and ingenuity. Staying involved with schools has kept our message sharp, the energy upbeat, and the kindness extreme. You have to be on your toes when you're speaking to 1400 screaming teenagers who'd rather be (initially at least) at a Justin Timberlake concert. School environments continually remind us of the power of humour when communicating the message of compassion.

At first blush, "kindness" sounds suspicious: "Are you trying to tell me I'm going to *enjoy* spending this sunny afternoon serving tea at the rest home?" Well, yes. And we've managed to convince people by showing them volunteering can be an adventure, invigorating, and fun. When we speak, we like to share the age-old insight that "it is only in the giving that we truly receive." Speaking to school groups has become a real passion for us and we are currently developing and presenting a curriculum that will help integrate kindness into the fabric of school life.

In the realm of business, our sponsors continue to set the standard for forward-looking, community-minded corporations. CHIP Hotels has certainly earned its title, "The Hotels with Heart," sending out employees on a regular basis to help at local soup kitchens and food banks. While we were on tour, SAS Canada unveiled a corporate initiative that pays every employee in the corporation for four days' work per year at the charity of his or her choice. Itsyoursole.com and Columbia Sportswear continue to sponsor progressive community-based initiatives that build bridges between people and communities. We thank them whole-heartedly for inspiring us, thinking outside the box, and keeping the dream of a friendlier planet alive.

Thanks to extensive media coverage, emails, and phone calls from as far away as Europe, Southeast Asia, and the Middle East, we have lived up to our promise to connect the world through kindness. As the *Pay It Forward* arithmetic suggests, by passing on a kind act and encouraging others to do the same, our work has made a positive difference (the extent of the difference is not important) in the lives of everyone we met. A compliment can make someone's day and a day altered can change the course of a lifetime.

Catherine Ryan Hyde joked at our press conference in Halifax, "No one is going to come along and tell you to stop." We have no intention of stopping now.

The Kindness Crew — Val Litwin, Erik Hanson, Chris Bratseth, and Brad Stokes — have taken on Canada!

ACKNOWLEDGEMENTS

Sponsors: Minaz Abji, Charlene Krepiakevich, Alasdair Douglas, and Kelly Van Sickle at CHIP Hospitality and all the Kindness Captains; Carl Farrell and John Quinn at SAS; Jeff Timmins and Doug Hamilton at Columbia Sportswear; Mike Baker at ItsYourSole.com; Karim Allibhai and Radiant Communications; Jim Hoggan at James Hoggan & Associates; Telus; Jamie Grimes and Jeremy Sheppard at Synergy; Rob Lowrie and Tanya Smith at CH; Dave Wheaton at Dave Wheaton Pontiac Buick; Rob Reid at Frontrunners; Naoya Kusano and The One Lounge; Leslie Anderson and Hal Douglas at Happy Planet; Frank Naccarato at Moxies; John Shields and everyone at the 100.3 The Q; Carmine Sparanese at Lifestyle Markets; ReBar and Steve Hanson, Norm and Michelle Isherwood, Steve Cox, Jon Curleigh, Jack Julseth, and Del Volk.

Helping Hands: the City of Powell River, Ash Varma and Viv Watson at the Powell River Rotary, the staff at Green Cuisine, Live to Surf, Sooke Cycle and Surf, Bill Weaver at Across Borders, Jeff from the computer lab at UVic, Shawn Dogimont from HoBO, and Dorothy from Freddy Beach.

Shining Stars: Deirdre Campbell, Catherine Ryan Hyde, Holly Whalen, The Hammer Family, Brock Tully, Vicki Gabereau, Russ Froese, Walt Nicholson, Nora Arajs, Karen Ammond, Arthur Black and Duncan McCue at CBC, Brent Gilbert at CTV, John Kehoe, Mark Litwin, Dale Mclean, and Joy Gugeler and Jack David at ECW.

Loved Ones: Christin and the Petelski family, Dale Mclean, Mark and Gethsemane Luttrell, Lauren Garvey and Christina Reti, Anne Larrass, Carl and Jacob Hanson, Sheel Tengri, Kendall Kelly, Graham and Tracy Sherman, Brennan and The Sinclair Family, Brian Green, Shandri Phillips, Julia Waring, Alym Hirji, Mike Graham, Joanne Gillies, Uncle Dave and Aunt Cory, Norma and Vern from Brandon, Mike Alyward, Rod Brown, Mike Hilleren, Mike Grey, Peni Puschmann, Josh Williams, Katherine and Kelly Manning, Jill Henry, Kim Oz, Ashley Gas, Nadine Marshal, Gail Schmidt, Ben Fox, Susan Garvey, John Garvey, Aunt Joyce and Uncle Will, Farah Nosh, Darren Bennett, Lance Moore, Erin Lee, Louise LaPoint, Brett Mcgilivrey, Donny in Fredericton, Len and Willie in Merritt, Henry in Lorette, Milan and his buffalo, Casper Boone, and Sonny Kapoor.

RECOMMENDED
RESOURCES

BOOKS

Colf, Mary, and Len Oszustowicz. *301 Acts of Kindness: A User's Guide to Giving Life.* Chelsea: Summit, 1994.

Community of Kindness. Boston: Conari Press, 1999.

Engwicht, David. *Street Reclaiming.* Gabriola Island: New Society, 1999.

Forsey, Helen. *Circles of Strength.* Gabriola Island, New Society, 1993.

Freedman, Marc. *The Kindness of Strangers: Adult Mentors, Urban Youth, and the New Volunteerism.* Toronto: John Wiley and Sons, 1993.

George, Don. *Kindness of Strangers.* Oakland: Lonely Planet, 2003.

Gould, Meredith. *Deliberate Acts of Kindness: Service as a Spiritual Practice.* Chippensburg: Destiny Image, 2002.

Green, Terri. *Simple Acts of Kindness: Practical Ways to Help People in Need.* Old Tappan: Revell, 2004.

Hicks Settle, Cheryl. *Sowing in Silence: 101 Ways to Sow Seeds of Kindness.* New Jersey: Sanctuary International, 1998.

Hopkins, Janet. *Common Kindness*. League City: Heartfelt Press, 2004.

Keefer, Sandra Lee. *The Power of Kindness: Learning to Heal Ourselves and Our World*. Writer's Club Press, 2001.

Kehoe, John. *The Practice of Happiness*. Vancouver: Zoetic Inc., 2001.

Kent, Susan. *Learning How to Be Kind to Others*. New York: PowerKids Press, 2003.

Kids Random Acts of Kindness. Boston: Conari Press, 1994.

Larned, Marianne. *Stone Soup for the World: Courageous Acts of Service*. New York: Three Rivers Press, 2002.

Lavasik, Lawrence. *The Hidden Power of Kindness: A Practical Handbook for Souls Who Dare to Transform the World, One Deed at a Time*. Manchester: Sophia Institute Press, 1999.

Maalouf, Jean. *The Power of Kindness*. Mystic: Twenty Third Publications, 2003.

Markova, Dawna, and Daphne Rose Kingma. *Random Acts of Kindness*. Boston: Conari Press, 2002.

Marx Hubbard, Barbara. *Conscious Evolution: Awakening the Power of Our Social Potential*. Novato: New World Library, 1998.

McIntyre, Mike. *The Kindness of Strangers: Penniless Across America*. Berkley: Berkley Publishing Group, 1996.

McKinley, Cindy, and Mary Gregg Byrne. *One Smile*. Bellevue: Illumination Arts, 2002.

More Random Acts of Kindness. Boston: Conari Press, 1994.

Pilburn, Sidney. *The Dalai Lama: A Policy of Kindness*. Ithica: Snow Lion Publications, 1993.

Pliskin, Zelig. *Kindness: Changing People's Lives for the Better*. Brooklyn: Mesorah Publications, 2000.

Power of Kindness: Reconnecting with Friends and the World. Boston: Conari Press, 2000.

Practice of Kindness. Boston: Conari Press.

Roddick, Anita. *A Revolution in Kindness*. London: Anita Roddick Books, 2003.

Ryan Hyde, Catherine. *Pay It Forward*. New York: Simon and Schuster, 2000.

Schecter, Fishel. *Loving Kindness: Daily Lessons in the Power of Giving*. Brooklyn: Mesorah Publications, 2003.

Shipka, Barbara. *Leadership in a Challenging World: A Sacred Journey*. Oxford: Butterworth, 1997.

Wagner, David. *Life as a Daymaker: How to Change the World by Simply Making Someone's Day*. San Diego: Jodere Group, 2003.

Williams, Linda, Susanna Palomares and Dianne Schilling. *Caring & Capable Kids: Activity Guide for Teaching Kindness, Tolerance, Self Control & Responsibility*. Carson: Jalamar, 2002.

WEB SITES

World Kindness Movement, www.worldkindness.org.sg

Kind Acts, www.kindacts.net

Random Act of Kindness Foundation, www.actsofkindness.org

Ananda Club, www.allbehappy.net

Canadian Kindness Movement, www.kindness.ab.ca

Small Kindness Movement of Japan, www.kindness.or.jp
Singapore Kindness Movement,
    www.singaporekindness.org.sg
Thailand Kindness Movement Foundation,
    www.thaikindness.com
Pan African Reconciliation, www.peace.ca/africa.htm
Kindness Scotland, www.kindnesscotland.co.uk
Australian Kindness Movement, www.kindness.com.au